A Parent's Guide to Divorce

A PARENT'S GUIDE TO DIVORCE

How to Raise Happy, Resilient Kids
Through Turbulent Times

Karen Becker, MA

ALTHEA
PRESS

For general information on our other products and services or to obtain technical support, please contact our Customer Care Department within the United States at (866) 744-2665, or outside the United States at (510) 253-0500.

Althea Press publishes its books in a variety of electronic and print formats. Some content that appears in print may not be available in electronic books, and vice versa.

Designer: Merideth Harte
Editor: Susan Randol
Production Editor: Andrew Yackira
Author Photo: Isabelle Korpela

ISBN: Print 978-1-64152-121-5 | eBook 978-1-64152-122-2

To Isabelle, Kacey, and Jordan
You are my inspiration to do my best.

Contents

Introduction

When parents are considering divorce, their focus turns
to the children. Will the kids be okay? Will the divorce have
long-term effects on them? These are normal questions for
parents to ask. From personal and professional experience, I
can tell you that divorce does not have to negatively affect the
children involved. Most children can and do thrive after their
parents' divorce and grow up to create their own happy families.
This book is meant to be a guide, helping you navigate the world
of divorce from a child-centered perspective so your children
can thrive.

As I finished my master's degree in counseling, one of my
professors told us that our niches in the counseling world would
develop naturally. When I started facilitating co-parenting
groups prior to graduation and through my own divorce, it
quickly became apparent that the world of divorced parents
is where I belonged. Since then, I've worked with hundreds of
families directly and have impacted thousands more indirectly
through co-parenting courses, books, and support groups.

Besides my professional work, I am a divorced mom to three
incredible biological daughters and one amazing bonus daughter. My supportive husband and I have created a happy, blended
family. Our transitions weren't easy, but our effort has been
worth it. My husband and I get to look at our daughters' happiness and successes with gratitude and pride.

While this book is a child-centered guide, I know the challenges parents face individually, too. Divorce is a complete upheaval of your life and everything you've known. My experience has taught me that co-parents cannot effectively work together until they face those challenges, so the first chapter in this book is dedicated to them. The bonus is that every tool you decide to use in that chapter also becomes a lesson in resilience for your children. By the way, you will notice that I often use the word *children* rather than *child* throughout this book; it is simply to make some of the discussions easier to read.

Divorced parents fall within a spectrum of low-conflict to high-conflict relationships. Wherever you are on the spectrum, this book will help you. It doesn't matter where you are in the divorce process. Maybe you're considering divorce or maybe you're signing papers. Either way, this book can be an excellent guide for you and your co-parent as your children navigate life outside of a two-parent home.

This book is divided into five chapters for each stage of divorce, and each chapter discusses various parenting topics by age group. Though infants are not specifically listed, know that the more communication between co-parents the better. Consistent schedules are key to an infant's development after separation and divorce. Bonding is an important part of infancy, so whenever possible, both parents need meaningful time with their infant.

Because this book is child-focused, you'll learn how to talk to your children about the divorce and related matters and what to look out for throughout the transition period and beyond. I'll talk about ways to handle any struggles your children are having, and because you know your children best, you may want to look into other age group discussions to identify any issues they may be dealing with that aren't listed with their age group. You'll also meet a few families throughout the book based on actual clients whose own personal situations can help you with yours. I haven't used anyone's real name, and I changed identifying characteristics for privacy.

Divorce isn't an end; it's a new beginning. Though this is a difficult time for you and your children, it's only part of your story. Many families come out of divorce stronger and closer than before. The goal of this book is to help you raise happy, resilient children. Resilience isn't the absence of difficult times; it's the skills and ability to get through them. All of those skills are learned, and this book is one of the resources to help you learn them.

I strongly believe that divorce is just a chapter in each of your stories, not the entire book. You hold the pen and have the opportunity to write the remaining chapters. I believe in family, however you define it. I wish you good luck and happiness as you get through this chapter of your lives.

Chapter One

Create a Parenting Plan

A parenting plan is a written set of guidelines and decisions to help co-parents work together as parents even though they're living apart. When you go through a divorce, you make decisions about who will have custody of the children (joint or sole legal and/or physical custody; who will make decisions on behalf of the children), placement (how the children's time will be split between the parents at the two homes), and financial matters regarding the children.

A parenting plan helps with the day-to-day issues that come up as you parent your children. How will you determine which extracurricular activities your children are involved in? Who will their primary care providers be? If the need arises, how will you decide on a specialist? Will you need to select a school? Think of a parenting plan as protection for your children, your co-parent, and you. The more detail you can put into a parenting plan, the easier it will be for you down the road because these decisions will have already been agreed upon. When you are ready to write your parenting plan, use the checklist in the Parenting Plan Checklist on page 123 as a guide.

Acknowledge Your Feelings, Concerns, and Fears

Before you can start a parenting plan, you'll need to address your own feelings. Too many co-parents go into building a parenting plan from a place of fear or anger. This results in arguments, delayed decisions, misunderstanding, and more hard feelings. None of this helps the kids.

Divorce is a change in everything you and your children know. It's a crisis for all involved, and because of that, you will go through all the emotions that come with crisis. Emotionally speaking, divorce is the end of the life you and your co-parent had planned for. When these endings happen, you will go through a divorce version of the stages of grief.

One of those stages is denial; you may ask yourself, "Is this really happening to me?" You may also go through the bargaining stage, wondering if you can make changes that could impact your decision to divorce. You may also go through a season of depression or sadness. And like most co-parents, you may find yourself in the anger stage at some point during the divorce process. In fact, many people are in the anger stage prior to announcing the divorce. Then, finally, after a divorce and putting in the healing work, you'll find yourself in a different mind-set where you recognize hope for a new future. That leads to acceptance, during which time you accept that divorce is only one part of your life story.

These stages of grief are not a direct line from one to the other; rather, they are stages you will go through in various orders and multiple times. Many co-parents report finding themselves back in the anger stage over and over again. To manage this, learn to identify the triggers that push you into the anger stage. Be aware of your own triggers, and then create a plan to manage them. This helps ensure you are doing everything you can to cooperatively co-parent—even when you're in a place of fear and/or anger.

Start wherever you are. Spend some time thinking about what your feelings are, right now, today.

- How do you feel about parenting with your ex?

- What, if anything, is holding you back from cooperatively parenting with your ex? What are your triggers? For example, do you boil up inside when you hear your children had toaster pastries for breakfast with your ex? Do thoughts of your ex cause an immediate negative reaction? A trigger can be anything.

- Do you feel you will be able to separate your feelings about your co-parent from that of making decisions for your children? If not, why not?

- What are your fears as you go through the divorce process?

While these questions are difficult to answer, they put you on the path toward healing because you're identifying the hard stuff ahead of time. You certainly won't be able to plan for everything, so I recommend revisiting these questions every year or so.

Now that you've identified the emotions that may hold you back from doing your part to cooperatively parent with your ex, it's time to put a plan in place to manage them. Here are three steps:

1. **Identify the emotion that comes with the trigger.** Name it. Acknowledge it. For example, as you prepare to talk to your children about the divorce, you may be feeling fear that they will be angry with you for the divorce.

2. **Allow yourself to feel your feelings.** Too often, we believe that we shouldn't feel negative emotions. "I shouldn't be sad."

"I shouldn't be so angry." The truth is, it's perfectly acceptable and completely normal to feel negative emotions. In fact, whatever you feel in this situation is justified and acceptable. As soon as you try to push back against the negative emotion, it will only push back harder. When you allow yourself to feel your feelings and they wash over you, you can move on to the next step and recover from them. You can allow yourself to feel the negative emotion through exercises like journaling, venting to a friend or family member, or even engaging in some artistic therapies. It's good to feel your feelings for a time to get them out of your system. The trick is to feel them without allowing them to interfere with your co-parenting. That leads to the next step.

3. **Redirect and let it go.** It's time to redirect after you've felt what you needed to feel. Expect to experience some emotional exhaustion once you've given yourself space to feel those difficult feelings. When you've hit that spot, it's time to let go and move on so you don't get stuck in that place of negativity. Listen to an upbeat song, do something active like going for a walk, or watch a funny video. It's safe to communicate with your co-parent when you've moved on, at least temporarily, from the painful feelings.

The reality is that divorce is filled with fear, anxiety, and frustration. If you're honest, the weeks and months leading up to the divorce were filled with those feelings, too. I don't believe anyone *wants* to remain in those hard emotional times, so it's up to you to do the work to heal. The trick to cooperation in building a parenting plan is to recognize and manage those emotions rather than react because of them.

While these are great steps to help you deal with your emotions, it's not possible to get to the hope and acceptance part of the stages without forgiveness. Forgiveness does not erase what's happened. It certainly doesn't excuse what's happened to get to the point of divorce. Forgiveness simply removes the power from it.

Think of forgiveness as a cleaning process. Imagine you're cleaning your closet, and you find an old sweater. As soon as you take it out of the closet, you are flooded with memories of the times you wore it. The sweater itself doesn't fit anymore and you know you need to get rid of it, but having this sweater in the back of your closet is all you've ever known. Now imagine this sweater is attracting moths, and the moths are ruining your newer clothes. It's easy to say it's time to get rid of the sweater, right? Sure, it leaves a hole in your closet, but tossing it also rids your closet of the pests.

This is forgiveness. Forgiveness is letting those hard feelings go. Forgiveness is ridding your life of the negative feelings that can ruin new memories. That hole in your closet? What would you fill it with? What about your life? When you rid yourself of the negative feelings by finally letting them go, you open yourself up to new thoughts and feelings. What thoughts and feelings will you put in the space you create?

Make Your Children Your Priority

This is a difficult time for everyone involved. It's important to make your children a priority, but it's hard to do that if you haven't spent time handling your own emotions first. As they say, put your own oxygen mask on first. Unfortunately, parents can get caught in a trap of unintentionally expecting their children to meet their needs during this time rather than parents meeting their children's needs. Children need both of their parents in their lives. For them to thrive during and after the divorce, they need structure, routine, and parents who are free of conflict.

Parents usually fall into certain roles in the marriage. Perhaps your co-parent put the kids to bed at night while you managed the meals. You may have always gotten the kids ready for school, but your co-parent did the pickups and the afternoon snacks. After divorce, both parents will have to take on each other's roles during their parenting time. One parent may believe that because they've always gotten the children ready for school, they should have the kids every morning to prevent change. This excludes the other parent from an important time in their kids' lives. While efforts can and should be made to keep routines as close to normal as possible, this can be done by teaching the co-parent a special routine. When you teach each other routines that are important to your children, you're giving your kids the gift of allowing them to love and count on both of you.

One of the hardest times for children of divorced families is the transition between the homes. Each house will have its own feel to it, but when each home has different rules and expectations, it's more confusing for the kids and harder for them to transition. Screen time, bedtimes, agreement on hygiene (e.g., brushing teeth and showering/bathing), and homework expectations are some of the issues I hear about often. Marcia is one example.

Marcia's parents were newly divorced. Marcia's teacher reached out to her parents to let them know that her homework wasn't as consistent as it once was. Marcia was a normal little girl who, when asked about homework, would evade the question or say it had been done. Marcia's dad went into her backpack each night and saw that the assignment notebook had assignments in it. He built "backpack time" into his nightly schedule so Marcia didn't have the chance to avoid the homework. Marcia's mom, on the other hand, was thrilled when she heard there was no homework because it gave them more time to do something fun, which they both loved. When Marcia's mom heard from the teacher, she realized her mistake and worked to fix it right away. Marcia's dad explained his "backpack time" to his co-parent, and she put that in place immediately. Marcia's mom made it part of "Mom and Marcia time" so neither of them missed out. Marcia's homework became consistent again.

Marcia's mom wasn't necessarily wrong in this case, but had the parents discussed things like this earlier, incomplete homework would not have been an issue. While details like this seem trivial or common sense to some, they aren't necessarily obvious to others. Whatever the case may be, they certainly aren't trivial for the kids. We can be quick to assume the other parent is on the same page, and the kids get caught in the middle. When kids have to remember different rules for different houses, they can become confused or exhausted.

As you consider your parenting plan, it's helpful to spend a day in your child's shoes. What does their routine look like? Routines can be taught and are important, but *structure* is a child's safety net. Though your child won't admit it, they want and need rules. These rules tell your children what to expect and prepare them for adult life. We have rules we need to follow at almost every point in our lives. There are rules for driving, expectations at work, and even rules for when bills are due. The rules we live by help keep us all safe, and the rules you and your co-parent create for your children will keep them safe.

Just as there are consequences when we break a rule (for example, fees when we pay a bill late or a speeding ticket when we don't follow the speed limit), you need to put consequences in place for when your children don't follow a rule. In an ideal situation, these consequences are followed through on at both houses. Decide with your co-parent on the rules and consequences, and don't forget the rewards when things are going well. In high-conflict cases or when parents simply don't agree on the consequences, it's possible for them to apply at only one of the homes.

Finally, but most important, the number one factor in a child's ability to transition well after a divorce is how well their parents get along. The weeks and months leading up to a divorce are likely filled with tension and arguments. In your child's mind, the divorce is supposed to be the end of that. When I talk about how to tell the children about a divorce in chapter 2, one of the most widely used scripts includes phrases like, "Mom/Dad and I have been having trouble getting along lately, and we've decided it's best not to be married anymore." Many children are relieved when they hear those words because, in their minds, it will end the conflict. Children love their parents more than anyone else in the world and the last thing they want to see is the two people they love most fighting constantly. If the message they receive is that divorce is the end of the arguing, then they should not be a party to any arguments that happen after it's announced.

The reality is that divorce doesn't end the arguments or tension. This is one of the most stressful times of everyone's life, and during stress, parents want to protect their children. The protection co-parents offer may look different. For example, one parent may think they are protecting their children by easing up on the rules, while the other parent thinks that enforcing the rules is doubly important at this time. While neither parent is wrong, this difference of opinion creates conflict between them. This type of conflict can feel worse than before the divorce because both parents are in protective mode. Making an effort to understand the other's point of view, managing your own fears while in protective mode, knowing there's no single right way to parent, and extending a little grace are all things you can do to ensure your children don't have to be part of more conflict. You only have control over yourself and what you do and say, so even when the other parent is being difficult, know that what you do to lessen the conflict is still important.

When it comes to making your children a priority in a parenting plan, consider each decision from their point of view. Looking through the lens of your children's lives can change your perspective. Listen to your co-parent during this time, too, because different relationships with your children offer different perspectives on their lives. It's not a competition to get the most in here. It's a collaboration that's meant to protect the children.

Communication Is Key

Communication is the key to co-parenting. You don't have to like the person you're communicating with, but you still need to communicate to protect your children. When communication isn't occurring or it's filled with conflict, your children can get caught in the misfire. Keep this in mind as you build your parenting plan. The following guidelines can help you develop effective, cooperative communication.

SPEAK CIVILLY

You don't have to like your co-parent, but you should make every effort to communicate civilly for your communication to be effective. Whether you're talking to each other, texting, e-mailing, or using a communication tool designed for divorced families (see Resources on page 126), communicate with your co-parent the way you would like them to communicate with you. If you feel yourself getting frustrated, take the steps listed at the beginning of this chapter, and do your part to manage your feelings rather than take them out on your co-parent.

After divorce, the communication with your co-parent will likely be limited to discussing issues related to your children. Remember that you and your co-parent may both be protecting what you believe are your children's best interests and that you are both likely coming from a place of fear and/or anger when communicating about these issues. Resolution comes when you remain calm, listen to your co-parent's point of view, communicate civilly, and stick to the facts.

SHARE INFORMATION

I can't stress enough the importance of both parents being involved in their children's lives. This lessens the impact of the divorce on them, and the transition is easier when their parents are on the same page. Parents can't be on the same page, however, if they're working with limited information. It's extremely important to share valuable information with your co-parent, so decide together what should be shared.

I recommend scheduling time at least every three months to discuss what each of you are experiencing with your children. For example, in mid-August, before the school year starts, look at the school calendar together. This is an opportunity to coordinate your children's days off from school, concerts, extracurricular activities, and breaks. Before winter break, you can check in with each other to discuss how your children have been doing in school and at home. Then, in February, you can make plans for the remainder of the school year, and circle back around a few months later as the school year winds down to compare notes. These are all good opportunities to discuss with your co-parent any vacations or staycations you want to take with the kids.

While planning the school year and summer is a great start, it doesn't take care of day-to-day life. If a child was getting sick while you still lived together, it was easy for both of you to see and start to plan for who may have to miss work. When both parents had an opportunity to review the test scores coming home, they were able to identify issues sooner. When you saw your toddler every day, you were able to watch and assess their development in real time. Now that you and your co-parent aren't seeing your children every day, comparing notes can fill in the gaps and create a more vivid picture of your children's lives. Therefore, it's important to continue to share information like this with your co-parent, even if communication is difficult.

PLAN LOGISTICS

Sharing information is important, but *what* information should be shared and *how* should it be shared? When you can agree on this in the parenting plan, it removes feelings of being left out and keeps both parents involved in their children's lives.

First decide on where/how to communicate. I am a personal fan of keeping everything in writing simply because it's easy to refer back to and prevents heated discussions later. If you decide to keep information sharing in writing, you'll need to decide if that means texting, e-mail, or using Internet tools like Our Family Wizard or coparently (see Resources on page 126).

Communication tools for divorced families can help keep both parents organized because there's a calendar, a place to list primary care providers, a section for finances, and a searchable e-mail system for communication outside of calendar updates. For some co-parents, communicating in writing feels impersonal so they'd rather keep it face-to-face. It's still a good practice to follow up a direct conversation with takeaways in writing just to ensure that you and your co-parent are on the same page. Make a decision based on what works for both of you, but consider a backup plan just in case. Even the most well-intentioned co-parents can find themselves in conflict. Supplementing the face-to-face interaction helps diminish the conflict.

Once you decide on what communication looks like, you will need to agree on what information to share. I've asked hundreds of co-parents, "What should you and your co-parent communicate about when it comes to raising your kids?" The answers vary, but in every case, they tell me they want as much information as they can reasonably get. In high-conflict situations, sharing information is the start to breaking down the barriers for your children. The list of must-discuss items should absolutely include:

- Medical and dental information

- Developmental information for babies (e.g., feeding and sleeping schedules)

- School information for older kids, including missing/late assignments, project work, and testing dates as the children get older

- Extracurricular information like practice schedules, game days, and equipment needed

- Any sudden changes in behavior

Once the must-haves are agreed on, consider the "nice-to-haves." Do you want pictures of your children every so often when your children are with your co-parent? (Some parents upload all the photos they take of their children to a shared folder on the Internet so the other parent can view them.) If you and your co-parent follow different religions or if one parent is more involved in the religion, do you or your co-parent want updates on any religion-related activities?

Here's an important one: Do you think you and your co-parent should exchange information about your children's friends, like their names, parents' names, phone numbers, and addresses? Would you like to know what your children are saying to your co-parent about their classmates and teachers? When you share information like this, you're less likely to be surprised by something you hear, and some of it is important information to have in case of an emergency. It's ideal for both parents to have access to the same set of information concerning other people in their children's life.

Divorce is such a jarring time for children. They're hearing news that their parents no longer want to or can be together. They're watching a parent move out of the home or may be moving out of the house themselves. Their time is suddenly split between their mom and dad rather than all their time being Mom's *and* Dad's. The best gift you can give your kids at this time and throughout their lives is to present a united front.

Rules and discipline aren't at the top of any child's list of favorites, but they are the number one way to make a child feel safe. After divorce, these become even more important. Still, parents may instinctively overcompensate for the divorce by being more lenient. You may notice that your kids start testing the boundaries to make sure this part of their life isn't changing, too. Everything else in their lives is changing, but rules and discipline don't have to. In chapter 3, you'll learn more about what rules and discipline look like spanning two homes. For now, know that hearing phrases like, "Your Mom/Dad and I agree that . . ." will be the security your children need.

Outside of rules and discipline, a united front also comes in the form of both parents being part of big conversations and both parents attending and being involved in school and extra-curricular activities. This happens when you work with your co-parent to share information. You and your co-parent can't be fully involved in your children's lives if you don't know what's going on. Put any harsh feelings aside to show your kids that both parents are there for them. While it's ideal to sit together at your kids' events, it's most important that both of you are simply there.

One Parent or Two?

When there's high conflict in the relationship, parents may try to avoid each other simply to avoid arguments, but the children are the ones who suffer in those cases. So what do you do about the conflict? How do you protect the children?

Building a comprehensive parenting plan is one way to avoid conflict. After divorce, much of the conflict comes from having to come together to make decisions. When decisions are already made, your only duty is to make the best of them for your children's sake. Conflict also comes up as the parties continue to heal. It will take work, but if you can recognize when the hard feelings take over, you can learn to compartmentalize those feelings as you focus on your kids.

If it doesn't seem likely for you and your co-parent to work together, splitting up what each of you handle can also prevent conflict. For example, one of you handles regular checkups at the doctor, while the other handles regular checkups with the dentist. Continue to share information, but prevent conflict by splitting the duties. Remember, this isn't a competition. Kids benefit when both parents are involved.

Somewhere along the way, it's likely that you or your co-parent will enter into a new relationship. Regardless of how amicable your divorce is, the news of your ex moving on will sting a little. Planning for this eventuality isn't going to be a fun conversation, but if you and your co-parent can get on the same page about when to introduce a new partner to your children, it can prevent conflict later.

A parenting plan is only good when it's followed. Work with your co-parent to build it, but then it's up to each of you to follow it. If your co-parent starts to veer off the plan, keep communication open, listen to their side of things, be empathetic and flexible, and keep the spirit of working together alive should you need to change things. Flexibility is essential throughout the divorce process and after, because no matter how robust and detailed your parenting plan is, not everything goes as planned. This doesn't mean you shouldn't work hard to build a solid parenting plan. Remember this, and build in a way to make decisions later if you need to make changes to the parenting plan.

BECOME A MODEL

Divorce is likely the first crisis your children will face. It's also likely to be one of the largest crises you will face. Remember, children will follow your example, not always what you say. The most important audience you'll ever have—your children—will be watching the way you handle this crisis and everything that comes with it (including hurt feelings, conflict, fear, and insecurity). I tell parents all the time that they do not have to show their children perfection; it's not attainable. They do, however, need to show their children that when life gets hard, there are healthy ways to cope with it. If you're feeling stuck, reread the beginning of this chapter and do the work; find support in family, friends, and/ or therapy; and know that your children are watching and learning from you.

Determine Goals

Many decisions you make as parents are based on the goals you have for your children later in life. Some parents decide to get their children involved in sports early to teach teamwork and dedication, whereas others will decide to teach multiple languages or instruments. Now that you're working toward building a parenting plan, the goals you have for your children can and should continue to drive decision-making.

Think about your short-term goals. You want your children to feel safe and loved by both of you all the time, but especially during this time. That safety and love comes in the form of having access to both parents. How can you ensure your kids have access to both you and your co-parent during this transition? This may mean a phone call or video chat to the other parent every day. Security and love also comes in the form of a united front. How will you and your co-parent communicate as you watch for clues on how the kids are handling the divorce?

When you consider long-term goals for your children, think about how those goals are going to play out in the parenting plan. Again, the goals are about safety and making sure your children know they are loved, but there's more to it when you think long term. While the initial transition may have worn off, your children's needs will change, especially as the years go on. Plan to check in with your children often, and build communicating about long-term goals into your parenting plan.

The purpose of goals for your children is not about removing the difficulty of your divorce, refusing to talk about it, or brushing over it. It's about healthy communication, boundaries, and solid parent-child relationships throughout the divorce and afterward. What can you do to facilitate and nurture those goals?

Know the Milestones

Your parenting plan must factor in your children's developmental milestones. Both goals and steps toward those goals depend on age-appropriate information. Here's what you need to know by age.

TODDLERS

At this age, it's very important for both parents to be on the same page when it comes to mealtimes, bedtimes, potty training, and expectations. Your toddler is going through an extraordinary period of development during these years—from learning to walk, run, kick, and jump to trying out new words and potty training. Communication about the developmental steps your toddler takes is especially key so you can stay on the same page and know what to expect.

PRESCHOOLERS

In the life of a preschooler, it's all about school and socialization. Structure in the home will keep your preschooler feeling safe and secure as they expand their horizons by attending school and meeting new people. This structure comes in the form of similar bedtimes and routines at both homes and handling homework and projects that might come home with them. Try to be flexible with playdates so your preschooler has the opportunity to get together with their new friends.

YOUNG CHILDREN

Young children are learning to handle schoolwork and everything that comes with being in school, but they're also starting to get involved in extracurricular activities. This is one of the times in your children's lives when they are driven by exploration and curiosity. Make sure your parenting plan includes a way to decide on which activities your children will participate in and how to handle it if they suddenly decide they don't want to participate anymore. Communicate about homework, tests, and other school-based issues, as well.

Peers and electronics rule the lives of preteens. During this time, parents need to agree on the same terms when it comes to social media and the expectations surrounding it. Watch out for bullying, both online and in person. Preteens will want to get together with friends, so set some ground rules for after school get-togethers and similar activities. Communicate with your co-partner about how your preteen is doing socially and emotionally.

TEENAGERS

Teenagers usually enjoy a little more freedom than younger age groups. They start spending time alone unsupervised, begin to date, and may eventually get jobs. Teenagers who have parents with similar rules at their homes feel more secure. On the digital news outlet Quartz, child psychologist Lisa Damour reports that "children need both affection and structure in order to develop into secure, happy adults." She goes on to say that if parents cannot provide both, they should provide structure. So this is the time to get on the same page about when your kids can be left home alone and for how long, who can be with them, and what other responsibilities they may be ready to take on.

YOUNG ADULTS

Young adults are on their own much of the time. Though they're off to college and branching out, they still need their parents for many things, but especially for financial support. Decide together how you will each be able to help out your young adult with this aspect of their lives. Though your decisions will be individual, it will help your children to know what to expect from each of you.

LONG-DISTANCE PARENTING

Long-distance parenting happens when one parent lives far enough away that the distance makes it hard to see their children on a regular basis. The distance, however, does not have to prevent the parent from being an active part of their children's lives. Consistency and communication are the keys to successful long-distance parenting. Set up a weekly time for a video chat and/or phone call, and use that time to do homework together, read books, or even play games! As your children grow, the time you spend together on these calls will grow, too. Throughout the week, sending quick messages to let your children know that you're thinking of them also keeps you involved. Many children with long-distance parents find comfort in stuffed animals, books, or cards that replay a loving message in their parent's voice.

A Childhood for Your Children

As co-parents, you both have ideas of what you'd like your children's childhood to look like. Whether those ideas include T-ball practices or microscopes, most parents can agree on one thing: children should have a childhood filled with positive memories. While divorce isn't something any parent plans for their children, it's a reality for many nonetheless. Many parents worry that divorce will rob their children of their childhood. But by following a few guidelines, you can ensure your children will have as normal a childhood as possible, even after a divorce.

As I've stressed, communication is important in co-parenting. Even though your relationship is over, communication is not. Since your time together is limited, it can be tempting to have conversations about the children at pickup or drop-off, but having these conversations in front of your children only results in insecurity on their part. These conversations can quickly lead to conflict, which the children do not need to see. Rather than talking together at this time, set up a later time to talk, whether that is after the children are in bed or through e-mail. Build your method of communication into the parenting plan.

In some high-conflict situations where communication is strained, parents can be tempted to use their children as the communicators. Some of these parents will outright ask their children to talk to the other parent for them, whereas others use their children's backpack as a communication device. This puts a lot of pressure on the children, knowing they are solely responsible for the communication between the parents. Mediators, family therapists, and some co-parenting communication programs can help these parents learn to communicate effectively and keep the children out of it.

It's painful for children to overhear negative talk about their mom or dad when their parents vent to their support system. Venting is a great way to get the frustrations you feel out of your system, but if your children are with you, assume they are always within earshot. You may need to wait to vent to someone until your children are with your co-parent.

NEVER MAKE YOUR CHILDREN TAKE SIDES

Not making children take one parent's side over the other's seems like common sense, but some children still feel put in the middle of their parents' divorce, sometimes without their parents even realizing it.

Asking children where they want to live or if they like their mom's or dad's house more are questions children should *never* have to answer. Even with the best intentions, these questions put pressure on the children, pressure they should not have to feel. Children must be permitted to love both of their parents, and while they'll bounce back and forth between being closer to their mom and closer to their dad, they will always love both parents. Just as questions about who your favorite child is seem unanswerable, questions about whose side the children take are just as unfathomable for the children. Even without outright asking the children whose side they're on, there are ways in which the children can feel put in the middle. Take the example of George and his parents.

George woke up screaming from a nightmare, and his mom ran into his room. George told her that he felt like he was trapped. His mom held him and showed him that his door was open and her bedroom door was open and said it would stay that way. George said that sometimes his dad closes his bedroom door when he's there because his dad is watching TV and doesn't want the noise to wake George. George's mom responded that his dad shouldn't do that and it was a very bad thing to do. She told George she would call his dad right away to tell him never to do that again. George loved both of his parents. He felt like he got his dad in trouble and that he was the reason his mom was so upset. George decided to try harder not to tell his mom things about his dad that would upset her.

Both parents' hearts were in the right place; they just wanted to protect George. This would have been a great opportunity for his parents to talk to each other to figure out how to help George manage his fears. Like in the case with George, a parent's reactions to what their children say about their time with the other parent can make them feel like they are in the middle, needing to take a side.

A neutral, loving reaction that encourages positive relationships will make your children feel safe and secure. In the case of George's mom, instead of focusing on what his dad was doing, she could have talked to George about his feelings by saying something like, "It sounds like you are scared when the bedroom door is closed. Is that right?" This response would have helped George feel heard. From there, his mom could have a discussion with her co-parent concerning George's fears and the closed bedroom door without putting their child in the middle.

SMOOTH OUT TRANSITIONS

Throughout the divorce process, everyone is in transition. One or both parents are moving, and a new schedule and routines are being created. Everyone is feeling a little lost. During this time, children need to feel secure. Just because their world is changing doesn't mean the people who love them are. Pickups and drop-offs may be difficult for the children. They may feel scared they won't see the parent they're leaving again, worried about forgetting something at one of the houses, or struggling with where they fit in now. Communication between co-parents during this time is important for security reasons. Whenever possible, have doubles of important items (for example, a favorite toy or stuffed animal) as this can limit the fear kids feel. If that isn't possible, make sure to communicate your plan with your co-parent if something is forgotten.

When pickups and drop-offs occur, the kids are resetting. Even if their mom and dad have the same rules and expectations at their homes, each home will run slightly differently. Each home will have its own set of sights, sounds, smells, and routines. Your children need to reset to your house each time they come back to it. Many kids go through this reset silently—and that's okay. Give your children space when they come home, reminding them that you're there when they're ready.

With that said, keep pickups and drop-offs free of conflict. As mentioned earlier, making sure adult conversations occur without the children around is a step, but know that even silence can feel like conflict to the children. Have you ever walked into a room where the people in it weren't talking to each other? The silence is deafening, isn't it? You can feel the tension. Your kids can, too. If you and your co-parent have a high-conflict relationship, it's much better to remain silent than it is to communicate, but whenever possible, offering a smile and a hello goes a long way in making the transition from one home to another positive for your children.

Childhood should be about fun, exploring, and learning, and this means your children need to feel safe, first and foremost. After a divorce, understand that they will explore and learn on their own time and in their own way. Offering support as they navigate their new world, ensuring they feel safe enough to love and build a bond with both parents, and giving them plenty of playtime ensures they will have a balanced childhood even after divorce.

Chapter Two

Separation Starts

Weeks and months' worth of discussions have led to the moment of your separation. This is the time when you are ready to announce the end of your marriage and the beginning of a new life as co-parents. I hope you have put a lot of thought and preparation into this moment, but even with all of that thoughtfulness and preparation, your children will still need to process this information their own way. There's no way around this difficult time, but there is hope.

Difficult times have a way of bringing people closer together and revealing strengths you didn't know you had. This chapter is devoted to helping you lovingly communicate the news of your separation to your children and understand and address their emotions.

What to Say to Your Children

This is the moment divorcing parents dread the most. Parents know that the news will be difficult for the children to hear, no matter their age. The good news is that the words you use can help reassure them. The way you present the information can let your children know that they are loved and supported in the midst of this life change. You know your children better than anyone, as well as your specific circumstances, so use the sample dialogues offered simply as a guide. When you have prepared what you're going to say, it's easier for you to be present for your children as you give them this news.

This conversation is best had with both parents at the same time. Even if you feel like you can't come together on anything else, try to do this together for your kids. Deliver the news in the marital home away from distractions. In an ideal world, the conversation happens when your children are at their best: rested, fed, and healthy. Life doesn't always work like that, though, so do the best you can. If you are unable to have this conversation together for any reason, the parent giving the news should not badmouth the other parent. Remember, your children love both of you. The parent who misses the chance to talk to the children should have a follow-up discussion with their children as soon as possible.

TODDLERS

Children in this age group need easy, simple-to-understand language filled with loving words for them. What these kids know is that they live in one house with their mom and dad. The word *divorce* isn't part of their vocabulary yet. They will need to know that they will still have Mom time and Dad time, and they will still have their toys and other favorite items. Toddlers learn through repetition, which means you and your co-parent will have to work together to explain the new living arrangement to them using similar language. Even after the original conversation, expect the same questions for weeks as your toddlers try to figure out what this means. Here's an example of what to say:

> *"Mommy and Daddy love you so much. Mommy and Daddy are having some hard grown-up problems, and we believe the way to fix that is for Mommy and Daddy to live*

in two houses instead of together in one house. Some days
you'll be with Mommy in your house with Mommy and
other days you'll be with Daddy in your house with Daddy.
We'll show you just what that means because we'll both
have calendars like this." (Wherever possible, have a calendar ready with simple language and/or colors showing
your toddler what day it is and who they will be with.)

PRESCHOOLERS

These children have probably noticed the arguing and have
felt the tension growing. This is a scary time for preschoolers.
They may have friends whose parents live in different homes. In
school, they're learning what "family" means, and they're beginning to understand that their peers' families all look a little
different. Much like with toddlers, this age group needs simple
explanations filled with love. Expect questions and reassure
them through loving reminders. Here's an idea of what to say:

"Mom and Dad have not been getting along very well
lately. We've decided that the best way to fix this is to
live in different houses. All of our problems have been
grown-up problems. We both love you so much, and we
want to make sure you still get special Mom time and
special Dad time. That means you'll have some days you
spend with Mom in your house with Mom and some days
you'll spend with Dad in your house with Dad. Both Mom
and Dad will still take care of you. We'll just be taking
care of you in different houses."

YOUNG CHILDREN

At this point in their life, many elementary school–age kids will
have a good idea of what divorce is. Language for these children
should be clear, loving, and filled with as much detail as you can

give them. Children in this age group are able to empathize and will be worried for you as their parents, but they will also be scared of what will happen to them. Here is an example of what to say:

> *"I'm sure you've noticed a lot of arguing between Mom and Dad lately. We're so sorry you heard us arguing. It makes us both sad that you heard it. We've had a lot of adult problems and have decided that the best way to fix it is to get a divorce. That means we are both still your mom and your dad, and we always will be, we will just be your mom and your dad in different houses. You will still have time with each of us. There will be days with Mom in your house with Mom and days with Dad in your house with Dad. You will still be going to school, you will have the same friends, and you'll still be playing baseball. Sometimes Mom will take you to practice. Sometimes Dad will take you to practice, but both Mom and Dad will be supporting you every day."*

PRETEENS

The preteen age is generally an emotional time of life all on its own. These kids are figuring out who they are, where they belong, and what that all means. Telling preteens about divorce should be more of a discussion than a monologue by one or both parents. Inviting discussion opens the door for communication later and helps these children feel safe asking difficult questions. They will want to know where they fit in throughout this process, so communication should be centered on them. As you ask them questions, make sure they know it's safe to answer honestly and that they will not get in trouble for the things they say. Remember, this is an emotional age, so expect a range of emotions and be prepared to handle them patiently and lovingly. Here is an example of what to say:

"I'm sure you've noticed a lot of fighting between Mom and Dad lately. We're sorry you've had to hear that. We've worked really hard to try to make it work, but we've decided it's best to get a divorce. It makes us sad to tell you this. What we do know is that we both love you so much, and we want to discuss this with you, knowing it's going to be hard. You will never have to choose between us or take sides. This decision to divorce is all about us. You've done nothing wrong. We're going to live in two different houses (explain who is moving out and when). *You'll still be going to school, playing sports, and seeing your friends. We think that this schedule* (have a schedule ready to show your preteen) *is what's best. I know some of your friends' parents have gone through a divorce. What do you want us to know?"*

TEENAGERS

It may seem as though teenagers are wrapped up in their own lives, but they're quietly perceptive. The news of a divorce may not be surprising to them. Many teenagers report that they could see it coming and were just waiting for their parents to tell them. Again, this will be more of a discussion than it will be a statement of fact that you are getting divorced. Teenagers need to know where they stand and how much this will affect their day-to-day life. Here's an example of what to say:

"We want to apologize to you for the tension and arguing you may have been witnessing. It's no surprise that we have been having trouble getting along. We've done everything we can to try to make this marriage work, but we've decided a divorce is the best answer."

Explain who is moving out, whether or not your teenager is attending the same school, and explain the schedule to them as well as when this all starts. End by asking them what questions or comments they have. Again, explain to them that it's a safe place for them to say what they need to, as this will keep the lines of communication open.

Many young adults live outside the home during school months and come home when they are on breaks. They may not have noticed the clues leading up to the divorce, so this may come as a surprise to them. They are figuring out their place in the world and come back to what they know as home only to find that home is changing. Be empathetic with this age group as the news may hit them harder than you'd think. At this age, it's important for them to know they can make their own decisions about where they will go. They'll process this news on their own time and in their own way. You and your co-parent should agree to respect your young adult's time frame. Here's an example of what to say:

"We're so happy to have you here, but we have some sad news. We have been having a hard time getting along lately. We've done everything we can to try to fix our problems, but we've decided a divorce is the best option for us. We want you to know that even though our marriage is ending, you have a home with each of us for as long as you want. Neither of us wants you to feel like you have to choose between us, so know we respect the time you spend with each of us."

A Separation Story for Others

Our kids just want to fit in with their friends. Though the divorce rate in the United States continues to stay in the 50 percent range, children may think that their parents' divorce separates them from their friends. There's a stigma attached to divorce. That stigma makes it hard for adults to tell others about divorce, but it can also make it hard for kids to tell others. As you talk to your children about the divorce, it can be helpful to give them ideas about what to tell people they know. Here are some ideas to help your kids talk about the divorce with others.

TODDLERS

A toddler's vocabulary grows on a daily basis, and many toddlers love to share the words they learn with anyone who will listen! While this can be funny at times, it can also be embarrassing when toddlers start to talk about their parents living in two homes. A toddler's social life is limited, so consider if it's necessary to help your toddler explain the divorce to others. If your toddler is a talker, this is a great time to talk about who to share private information with.

If your toddler attends daycare, ensure the staff is aware of the news so they can watch for changes in behavior. Here's an example of what to say to your toddler:

"We wanted to make sure you knew this right away. We're telling Grandma and Grandpa next and will let your teachers at daycare know. If your friends ask, it's okay to tell them that Mommy and Daddy are still your mom and dad, but we will live in different homes, but you don't have to tell strangers; they don't need to know."

PRESCHOOLERS

When preschoolers get together, they talk about the games they're playing as well as what their family is doing. Many times teachers will ask how the kids are feeling each day in school. Your preschooler may be feeling sad about the news and will likely share that. Make sure the staff knows the situation so they can be prepared and can help watch for any change in behavior. When it comes to talking to their friends, you can help your preschooler figure out what to tell them. Here's an example of what to say:

"Some kids say it's hard to talk about their parents' divorce with their friends. Do you ever feel like that?"

Wait patiently for them to answer. If they answer no, praise them and encourage them to talk to you about it if they ever wonder what to say. If they answer yes, then you can help them with a script, along these lines:

"Sometimes kids whose parents get a divorce feel like they're not the same as their friends because their mom and dad live in different houses, but when they find out that every family looks different, it really helps them. You still have a mom and a dad and always will. Does that help?"

Your preschooler isn't going to just talk to their friends, however. They will talk to their teachers, their friends' parents, or any other adult that they feel close to. Here's an example of what to tell them:

"Your teacher might ask you how you're doing. I want you to know that it's okay to tell your teacher that your parents are divorcing. It's okay to tell the people close to our family what's happening in our lives. Do you feel like there is someone you would want to talk to about the divorce?"

Wait for them to answer, and use the guidelines offered earlier to help them talk about it. The goal with your preschooler is to help them understand that it's acceptable to talk about the divorce, as long as it's with the trusted people in their lives.

Much like in the preschool world, elementary school teachers need to know about the divorce so they can be prepared. Young children may try to lean on their friends, but at this time in life, their friends may not know how to best support them. They're all still learning. They may also be afraid to tell their friends about the divorce, fearing it will impact their friendships. Ask your children if they've told their friends about it. If they haven't, ask if they'd like help with what to say. If they are willing to accept your input, help them come up with their own version of a statement like this one:

> *"My mom and dad are getting a divorce. It means my mom is moving into a different house. I'm sad that they won't be together anymore, but I still get to go to school here and now I get to decorate a second bedroom at my other house."*

Preteens are looking to fit in, and they might think their parents' divorce sets them apart from their peers. They want to make plans with their friends, but they are still learning a new schedule and aren't sure who to ask. They're figuring out how they fit into life with their mom and dad now that they aren't together anymore, and it's all confusing. Chances are good they've told their closest friends about the divorce. For those preteens who are moving away as a result of the divorce, this can be particularly hard to tell their friends about. Help your preteen come up with ideas, such as:

"My parents are getting a divorce. They're selling the house and getting their own houses and that means I'll have to go to a new school. I wish I could stay here, but my parents tell me that they have to move. They say I can visit since I'm not moving too far. Can we still be friends?"

If your preteen isn't moving away, it may still be hard for them to tell their friends simply because they're worried about fitting in. Here's an example of a discussion you might have with your preteen:

Parent: *Have you thought about what you'll tell your friends about the divorce?*
Preteen: *No.*
Parent: *Do you want to hear what other kids have said to their friends?*

Wait for an answer; if it's yes, then proceed. If your preteen doesn't want ideas, it can help to tell them that you're in contact with the guidance counselor at their school and that it's okay to ask them for help.

Parent: *Some preteens just come out and say it and wait for their friends to ask questions. Some kids have their friends over and talk to them outside of school. Do you think either of these are something you'd like to do?*

This is one of the hardest ages for children. Preteens can be plain old mean to each other. Because their goal is to fit in, some preteens use the ways that others stand out to propel their own social life. This is part of bullying. Divorce could potentially make your preteen stand out. Your preteen may also get extra attention because of the divorce, and this may make others jealous of them. If you fear that they may be affected by this, talk to the guidance counselor at your preteen's school. Explain the situation and your fears. Let them be an advocate for your child when you're not there, but if you do hear that kids are using your divorce to make your preteen's life more difficult, here are some suggestions:

Parent: *I am so sorry that these kids are saying the things they are saying. It's not your fault that we are divorcing. Can we talk about different things you can say to stop their comments?*
(Wait for them to say yes.)
Parent: *Tell these kids that it's not your fault that your parents are divorcing. You can tell them that every family looks different, including theirs. You are an example of how to stand up to bullying, and you're not alone. You can remind them that half of parents divorce and that you're not alone. You can also talk to your teachers and your guidance counselor so they can talk with these kids in their office.*

Let your preteen know that they aren't alone. Help them recognize all of the support around them. Your preteen wants to feel independent and wants to feel like they can handle this, but letting them know that it's a good idea to get support when they need it can take some of the pressure off.

TEENAGERS

Life for teenagers revolves around social activities. Interrupting their social life can be hard on them. When it comes to talking to their friends about the divorce, help them decide what to say. Remember that your decision to divorce may not be news to your teenager, so their friends might already have an idea that the news is coming. Help your teenager by making sure they understand the schedule so they can continue making plans with their friends.

While teenagers may feel more comfortable talking to their peers about the divorce than other age groups, they may struggle with what to say to adults. Teachers, bosses, and even their friends' parents may ask questions. Here is an idea for something you might suggest your teenager say to the adults in their lives:

"My parents decided to get a divorce. We're working out all the details right now so I can't really talk about specifics, but my parents can answer questions if you have them."

YOUNG ADULTS

At this point, this age group has the peer discussion down, but their friends' parents may ask more questions of your young adult than they'd ask of you. Whether it's intentional or not, this puts even more pressure on the child. I advise parents to have a script ready for their young adults to tell others who don't really need to know the details. This script should help shut down gossip and avoid any awkward situations. It should be short, sweet, and to the point, like this:

"My parents decided to divorce. I don't know the details, but I hope it leads to happiness for both of them."

Addressing Emotions

As you go through divorce, you're dealing with your own set of emotions. The cycle of fear, sadness, anger, confusion, and hopefulness you may be experiencing can feel overwhelming. Everything your co-parent does or doesn't do might seem to take over your every thought. It's during this time you and your

THE DIVORCE STAGES OF GRIEF

Just like parents go through a divorce version of the stages of grief, your children will also go through their own stages of grief. These stages will include fear, sadness, anger, confusion, and hope. The stages of grief are not a continuum. Kids will not start at one and end at the other. They will feel all of this, sometimes all at once, and will go through some of it over and over again throughout their adolescent lives. Know that this is okay. You're their guide through it all.

So how might some of these stages of grief play out? Take a look:

Children are scared of not knowing where they fit in and whether or not a parent will also leave them. Many children, especially the younger ones, are afraid their mom or dad will divorce them too. They are sad that the family they've known has broken up and are angry that it happened. After all, in a child's mind, why couldn't you just make it work?

During transitions, kids can feel confused about what's happening and where they're going. Though the marriage ends, conflict doesn't, and the kids are confused about what to say or do to help. They may feel unsure of who to ask to sign permission slips, who to tell when their friends want to hang out, or who to talk to about extracurricular activities.

Finally, after seeing the two people they love most in the world arguing and so unhappy, they're hopeful for a brighter future with less conflict and happiness for their parents. Just as parents want happiness for their children, children want happiness for their parents, too.

co-parent need to help your children process everything that's happening, too. Just as much as there is change for you, there's even more for the children involved. Depending on their age, this section offers some ideas to help you help your children address their emotions.

Regardless of your children's age, you'll need to look out for some common red flags that will tell you your children aren't processing emotions in a healthy way. These include:

- Regression in behavior (for example, wetting pants in a previously potty-trained child, using baby talk when they weren't, and wanting to co-sleep when they were independent sleepers)

- Sudden outbursts or big changes in behavior in a previously well-behaved child

- Changes in eating or sleeping patterns

- Difficulty managing emotions (for example, crying more than usual and suddenly becoming aggressive)

Be on the lookout for any major changes in your children's behavior, words, and actions. If you see changes, it may be time to bring in the professionals. Many therapists are trained to work with children whose parents have divorced. Whether you decide to use a therapist or not, it's always a good practice to have conversations with your children about their feelings.

TODDLERS

Start with getting on the floor to play with your toddler. When you're in their space, they're much more likely to talk to you than if you were to ask them to step into yours. While you're playing, ask them questions, such as "Does it feel strange to spend time with me without Mommy here?" or "Do you ever feel scared?"

Keep the questions simple. Wait patiently for the answer and respect it.

For this age group, books like *Dinosaurs Divorce* by Marc Brown and Laurie Krasny Brown and *I Have Two Homes* by Colleen LeMaire and Marina Saumell are great ways to open up conversation with your toddler. Hearing about others in a similar situation, even if it's fictional, helps toddlers feel less alone, gives them the vocabulary to talk about how they're feeling, and does so in a neutral way. TV shows like *Daniel Tiger's Neighborhood* and *Sesame Street* are giving voice to the changes in life and are examples to children about how to handle those times. Use these as conversation starters and tailor the specifics to your situation.

PRESCHOOLERS

At this age, children have more words to use to describe their feelings. Words like *happy, mad, sad, glad,* and even *frustrated* are regular parts of their vocabulary. Though they know these words and what they mean, they may not know how to respond when they feel these emotions. Some parents think it will make their children feel bad if they were to bring up the hard emotions, but it's really the opposite. In my experience and that of other therapists, bringing up the hard emotions lets your children know it's okay to talk about them, and it opens the door to talk about how to deal with them.

Simply ask your preschooler, "What made you happy today?" or "Is anything making you sad or angry today?" These types of questions show them you care and you're willing to listen to their answers. When they give you their answers, that's a great opportunity to talk about how *you've* handled situations like that in the past. For example, you can say, "Sometimes that makes me sad, too. When I feel sad, I like to play my favorite song and think of happy things. Would you like to try that, too?" The books and shows listed for toddlers can also help preschoolers handle this life change. They are also wonderful conversation starters.

YOUNG CHILDREN

This age group may have more to say than their younger counterparts. They're much more in tune with how they feel, which is a good thing. I'm a huge fan of using books, TV shows, and movies to open up discussion with your children. Fictional stories are excellent icebreakers and can make your child feel less alone in what they're feeling.

There's no greater movie about difficult life changes than *Inside Out*. In the movie, Riley's parents move across the country for a job opportunity. Riley has to deal with a new school and feeling accepted, a new house and a new room, and leaving her old friends behind as she makes new ones. Though this movie isn't about divorce, there are certainly many parallels, and the emotions Riley feels will be similar to how your child is feeling.

Watch the movie with your child and then talk about it. You can say something like, "I know this isn't the same as the divorce, but it does talk about big, scary changes. How do you think Riley handled them?" At the end of the movie, we learn that the only way to start to heal is to allow sadness to do "her" thing. We need to feel sad for a time to bring joy back. This is a great opportunity to tell your children that it's okay to feel sad and that you'll be there for them. You can also talk about ways to bring the joy back.

PRETEENS

This age is all about testing independence. Preteens want to hold on to the innocence and simplicity of childhood *and* explore and grow into their teenage years. Getting this age group to open up will take time and a lot of trust on your children's part. They need to know that it's normal to talk about emotions, that what they say won't get them in trouble or hurt someone else, and that what they say to you is confidential.

In my experience, many parents opt for a therapist during this stage because it's often easier for preteens to talk to a neutral party than to their parents. Whether or not you decide to enlist the help of a therapist, it's important to check in with your preteen regularly on how they're feeling. These check-ins should be enjoyable even when talking about tough subjects. Once a month or so, make a special dessert, create a no-technology space, and sit down to talk. Talk about the good, the bad, how each of you is doing with the changes, and how you can make the best of it.

At the first discussion, set down some ground rules like:

- Technology is turned off or put away during the discussion.

- No questions are off-limits. (However, if the truth portrays one of the parents in a negative light, answer questions in a neutral way without details.)

- Whatever is said during the discussion won't be repeated to anyone else.

- No one is in trouble for what they say, even if it's hard to hear.

- Everyone is respectful, open, and appropriately honest, even if it's hard.

Decide together with your children on the rules for your talks. This is important not just to help your preteen through the divorce process, but to keep your communication open as life gets more challenging for them. Hopefully everyone will walk away feeling a little better each time you have these discussions.

Communication with teenagers about their emotions is going to depend on the relationship you have with them. If you've built a relationship where they already talk to you, this won't be as challenging. If you and your teenager usually don't talk about emotions, think of this as a fresh start. It's an opportunity to create new lines of communication.

Spending one-on-one time with your teenager is a great start. Offer to take your teen for lunch and head to a local coffee shop. Once there, share with them that this is your way of starting a new tradition where you guys check in with each other. Tell them that you want to know how they're doing and if they've processed the divorce news. Assure them that no matter what they're feeling, it's okay. Instead of asking questions like "Are you doing okay?" that might elicit a single-word response, ask open-ended questions like "What are you thinking now that you've had a few days since we told you about the divorce?"

Getting your teenager to open up about their feelings may be a slow process. Keep at it. Some teenagers need to know that they're worth the fight. They need to see their parents consistently work before they feel comfortable totally opening up to them. Their lives revolve around their friends. They've worked through independence and have been building their own lives, naturally separating a little from their parents. It's a good practice to let them know from time to time that you're there to listen and be there for them, not just when it's divorce-related. However, the process of opening up must be at their own pace.

YOUNG ADULTS

If your young adult has moved away to college, you're probably only seeing them on breaks. Conversations are a little more difficult when it's over the phone or video chat, but not impossible.

Though they're starting to build their own lives, you are still their parent and this news does affect them. Don't be afraid to ask the simple question, "How are you doing with the news?" Be prepared for the answer, but don't be afraid of the question. They're working on finding their place in the world, and in the middle of that, their concept of home is changing. Just as this is a new start for you, it can be a new start for your relationship with your young adult.

Understand that your young adult may be angry with you. They understand more about divorce than their younger counterparts, and anger is a common emotion with this age group. You may have to start the process of rebuilding your relationship with your adult children. Be appropriately honest with them and keep making efforts to build your relationship, but respect their space and the time they need to rebuild.

Settling into Two Homes

This is when the reality of divorce sets in for all involved. As soon as someone moves out, it's real. The challenge here is making sure both homes feel like home to your children. Even if one of you is staying in the marital home, it won't feel the same without everyone living under the same roof. The parent who moves out of the marital home has their own set of challenges to make their new place feel like home to the kids.

If you are the parent who leaves the marital home, take steps to create a safe place for your children to make the transition easier. Regardless of your child's age, keep these two tips in mind:

1. Remember that the people you bring into your home are people your children will be interacting with. Choose wisely. With that said, home isn't about the things that are in it;

TOUGH QUESTIONS,
COMPASSIONATE ANSWERS

Inevitably your children will have questions about the divorce. Some questions will be appropriate to answer but others won't. Sometimes children want the answer, but sometimes they're asking just to make sure the same thing won't happen to them. For example, when a child asks, "Don't you love Mommy anymore?" they may actually be asking, "Will you stop loving me, too?" Here are three of the most common questions and appropriate answers:

Question: What happened?

Answer: *We had a lot of adult issues that we couldn't work out. Sometimes adults just go two different ways and have to decide if they can find a way to come together or not. We could not, and I'm sorry for that.*

Question: Will you get back together? (Or: What if Daddy still loves you?)

Answer: *I know this is really hard and scary. I want you to know that Mom and Dad will always be your mom and dad, and we will never, ever stop loving you. In the end, it's going to be okay, but through this, we're in it together. We're still a family. It just looks a little different now.*

Question: Why couldn't you guys just work it out?

This question takes courage because it's coming from a place of anger. Be patient and respect that it's okay for your children to feel angry.

Answer: *I know how hard this is. We didn't make this decision lightly. We tried very hard to work things out, but sometimes things don't work out the way we want or expect them to. We're forced to make the best of it after that. I'm sorry that this is happening. It's not what anyone wanted, but I know we can work together to make the best of it.*

it's about the people in it. Be there with them as they're settling in.

2. Moving out might feel like you're getting your freedom back, but remember that you are a parent first. Your children are watching and learning from you, so do what you need to do to heal, but remember that if your children are with you, they see what you are doing. Some of what you consider exercising your freedom may have to wait until they aren't around.

Whether or not you are the one leaving the marital home, you will likely have to learn something new to make this easier for your children. For example, you may need to learn how to braid your daughter's hair or take a class on making basic home repairs. When we look at what helps children transition to two homes, consistency is key. No one knows it all, so don't feel ashamed if there's something you need to learn. It takes a village, and most villages have a teacher. It's a great lesson for your kids when they see their parents admit to not knowing something and then working to learn it.

As you work to build two homes, some items will have to go back and forth between the homes, but having a child pack a suitcase a couple of times per week is asking a lot. Both homes should have sets of clothing, books, and toys. Your children may want to bring certain clothing items back and forth for playdates, sports, or special events, but each home should have its own general wardrobe.

If you are staying in the marital home, one of the challenges you'll face is the quiet and emptiness the kids feel without your co-parent there. While the parent who moves out is dealing with making a new home, you will have to address and manage the quiet and emptiness. Many kids report that the worst part of staying in the same house is how empty it feels. Though redecorating may not be in your plans, creating new routines will be. Be consistent with rules like bedtime and expectations for things like doing homework, but if your co-parent always watched the six o'clock news, that may be a difficult time for the kids. Be aware of your children's emotions at that time. For instance, you may decide to watch the news or create a new routine when six o'clock rolls around.

The second house will not always be the same size as the first. Sometimes one of the parents moves into an apartment or into a smaller home, and the children have to share a room when they're there. If your children are sharing a room, focus on the positives. Help your children come up with ways to share the space and help them see that they have their sibling right there with them part of the time. For younger children, this can be exciting, but as your kids age, they're more focused on privacy.

Privacy doesn't have to go away just because your children are sharing a room. Help your children come up with reasonable rules for their new room. Perhaps each of them can get the room to themselves for an hour every day, and you can post a schedule outside the room. Remind them that it's reasonable to ask each other before using their sibling's things and that they should give each other privacy when changing clothes (or they can use the bathroom to change).

A child's room is their space. They take this seriously. If they're sharing a room when they haven't before, the adjustment will be difficult in the beginning. Your children will be learning together so expect a little discomfort early on. Use the situations that come up as learning experiences and keep focusing on the positives.

The following suggestions will be most beneficial to the parent who moves out, but they can be helpful to either parent as you recreate your home for you and your children.

Creating a toddler-safe home can be challenging. Start with the basics: cover outlets, fasten cupboard doors, keep poisonous substances out of reach, install baby gates for stairs, and put sharp knives and tools in a place toddlers cannot reach. Once you've toddler-proofed your new home, work to make it feel like home with familiar colors, toys, and your toddler's favorite items like a stuffed animal or blanket. Some parents opt to purchase the exact same bed sheets and comforters for the two homes to make the transition easier for this age group.

If your child has a favorite stuffed animal or blanket, it's ideal to have one of each of the favorite comfort items at both homes, but if it's not possible, make sure those items go back and forth. Keep bedtimes, bedtime routines, and mealtimes consistent whenever possible. Children of this age will be potty training. These toddlers will see the most success when both parents follow the same routines. Safety and security come in the form of consistency here. Toddlers can find safety and security in two homes when you compromise on what consistency looks like.

PRESCHOOLERS

While there are fewer constraints for children of this age than there are for toddlers, it's still important to maintain consistency. In school, preschoolers have a consistent schedule every day. This makes them feel secure because they know what to expect. The same is true for what to expect in their new home. Again, keep bedtimes, bedtime routines, bath night, and mealtimes consistent in both homes.

Children in this age group may still have a favorite stuffed animal and/or blanket. It's important to either have one of each at both homes or to have it travel back and forth in a backpack.

Pickups and drop-offs may occur at school, so it's likely their backpack will hold the special items.

Give your preschooler a chance to express themselves when they move into their new room. They may want things to be exactly the same as they are at the other house, and that's okay. But if they don't, the transition can feel a little less stressful when you take them shopping to pick out items like new sheets and blankets.

YOUNG CHILDREN

There's a little more flexibility with this age group. They're able to handle differences between the homes in terms of how they look, but to make this transition easier, try to keep a consistent schedule and similar routines. Many kids this age enjoy having the opportunity to express themselves in different ways in each of their bedrooms. For example, at their home with Mom, their bedroom may be decorated in bright, bold colors, but at their home with Dad, they may choose to decorate in more neutral tones. This is a chance for *them* to create a space that makes them feel at home.

Home is about who is there with them, so include an area in your home where you and your children can interact. In this area, have some games, toys, and books; these are excellent tools to keep your children busy and offer opportunities to interact with them.

Children are going to test their limits at both homes. As I mentioned in chapter 1, having a parenting plan in place and following its guidelines shows your children you are a united front even though you're living in different places. Give your co-parent the benefit of the doubt if your children say something like, "Mom lets me stay up until nine o'clock now!" Testing routines is their way of making sure the rules haven't changed, too.

This age group will definitely want a say in which of their items goes to which house and what each of their rooms looks like. They may want to help you decorate or redecorate. Their belongings are part of their lives. Though it may not look like much to you or me, a preteen's room is filled with memories and opportunities.

Preteens will want to decide where their things end up. Don't be discouraged if they want to keep the majority of their belongings at one house. Give your preteen time and space, and keep communication open. Before long, both rooms will be filled with items that are special to them.

When your children move into their new room, give them a chance to express themselves as much as possible and engage in conversations about what can help their new room feel like home to them. Simply asking the question can make them feel special and hopeful about the future. Again, consistent rules and routines are key to successful transitions.

TEENAGERS

If you've lived in one house for a long period, your teenager will feel fairly established there. That doesn't mean there won't be the same sense of belonging at a new place, but understand that it may take a while. A teenager's life is filled with change. Between going through puberty and talking about what life is like after high school and preparing for it, many teenagers feel like life moves fast. A move like this adds to the changes already happening in their lives, but that doesn't mean it can't be exciting, too.

Allow teenagers the chance to express themselves and ask them what they need for the new place to feel like home. Let them help you decorate the entire home. Many teenagers feel like their opinion is undervalued, so this is a great opportunity to show them the opposite. They've likely watched friends go through similar experiences and were probably prepared for something like this to happen. Ask for their thoughts and opinions, but always maintain the parent-child relationship. Balance comes in the form of consistent rules and expectations between the two homes.

YOUNG ADULTS

This is a tough age group because their room at either house may be temporary (since they're often home only on breaks from college). Depending on where they are in life, both co-parents will want to create a space for them, but be realistic about what that looks like. Talk to your young adult about their plans and what they'd like to see happen with their belongings. If you feel that asking them questions like that puts them in the middle, keep their stuff where it is (when possible) and tell them what the plan is. While a parenting schedule may not be necessary for this age group, a discussion about what a space looks like for them is.

Your separation/divorce is one of the biggest transitions your children will have to make. They have learned the news of your divorce, they will be watching one of their parents move out or they may be moving to a new home themselves, and then they will have to settle into living in two different places and dividing their time between their parents. Be realistic with your expectations and watch for the red flags mentioned earlier in this chapter. Difficult times during this stage are common, but when you remain child-focused and communicate openly and effectively throughout the transition, you will all come out okay on the other side.

Chapter Three

During the Divorce

Your children are living in two different homes at this point, and have transitioned through the initial news of your separation and divorce. This stage comes with its own set of challenges like building routines, figuring out day-to-day logistics, making plans for holidays and special events, and the rules of discipline between homes.

You've created all the right tools like your parenting plan and have started to address your children's emotions throughout the transition. At this stage, you'll be building on the solid base you've already created, and you'll use what you've learned throughout to guide you.

Making Two Homes Truly Home

As you've read, a home isn't just a roof over your head; it's the people in it. With that said, home is also where your children go after school, and it's one of the places they hang out with their friends. Though your children probably aren't a fan of it, it's also where you give out chores and establish your expectations for acceptable behavior. Each age group has a different set of needs.

Though you'll learn about transition days (pickup and drop-off) and how to make them easiest for your children in each age group, if you are in a high-conflict co-parenting situation, here are special tips for you regardless of your children's ages:

- Either meet in a mutually agreed-upon location between your homes like a gas station or restaurant parking lot or use what's called curbside pickup and drop-off (at the co-parent's home). In high-conflict cases, any interaction can create more conflict. If you are in a public place, you are less likely to engage in conflict, but you don't have to be tied to a public place if there is no history or fear of abuse. In a curbside handoff, the parent who is dropping the children off at the co-parent's home remains in the car or gets out for a quick good-bye hug, but does not go up to the door. The parent who is starting their placement time holds the door open for the children, but does not go to the car. This prevents conflict in front of the children.

- If your children are old enough, let them carry anything that needs to go back and forth. If they aren't old enough or able to handle that, simply leave the items as close to the door as possible without having to engage in conversation with your co-parent. The parent who is starting their placement time should use this time to give hugs and get the kids inside as the other parent leaves.

- If you do find yourselves face-to-face, a simple smile or hello is all that's needed. Commit to keeping communication in writing so you don't find yourself in an argument in front of your children. Silence can be deafening for your children, but if you cannot manage a smile or a hello, silence is the answer.

Next, let's look at ways your children can feel more a part of your house. The initial transition from one home to another is most important, so the following sections discuss how to do that smoothly first. Then, it's on to chores. A great way to make your home feel like home is to assign chores to your children, but many parents wonder what their children can handle. With that in mind, I highlight reasonable tasks for each age group. Of course, it's also important to give your children opportunities to socialize in your home, so I discuss playdates, too, and why they're important. I offer tips to ensure both parents get the chance to host them.

TODDLERS

If your toddler is not in daycare, handoffs will likely happen at your homes. Pack anything that needs to go back and forth like a special blanket or stuffed animal, and let your toddler pack whatever they'd like to bring, as well. Your toddler may love their trucks and cars one day and trains the next. If they ask to bring a toy to their other parent's home, this isn't personal. Your toddler simply wants to play with the toy they're most interested in wherever they are.

It's important for your toddler to have a say in what goes back and forth, but toddlers can get carried away. It's okay to limit what your toddler brings to two to three items. Remember, each home should have its own set of toys and books so your co-parent's home will have plenty for them to do.

At this age, especially soon after the divorce, your toddler may have a hard time during these transitions. Each home feels different even if you work to make their bedrooms look the same and keep the same routines. Many toddlers will cry and say they don't want to go to their other parent's place, but as soon as they're with the other parent, they're happily playing.

The easiest way to help your toddler through difficult transitions is to have a drop-off and pickup routine. Make this routine quick and loving rather than drawn out. Give a hug, a kiss, and an "I love you" and hand your toddler off to their other parent.

Wave and say good-bye. I know how difficult this is to do if your toddler is crying, but drawing it out actually makes it harder on them. Know that they will be okay and that this is part of their learning that you aren't leaving them permanently and you'll always come back. It will get easier over time.

Toddlers can and should be a part of day-to-day activities like cooking and cleaning. At this age, your children can pick up their toys, put their clothes in a hamper, put clean clothes away, and help you in the kitchen with stirring and pouring. While these chores won't be completed quickly, giving your toddlers something like this makes them feel like a part of the household and increases their self-esteem. For extra fun, try singing a cleanup song with your toddler as you clean. (You can find songs about cleaning up for this age group on YouTube.)

At this age, playdates are common. Inviting friends with their own toddlers to your home is one of the easiest ways to make your children feel like this is home. If you don't have friends with children of similar ages, you can meet other families by attending story times at your local library, taking classes at a rec center in your town, or through religious institutions in your community. Your home is your toddler's home and that means friends will become a part of their lives there. Start young and watch as these friendships mature over time.

PRESCHOOLERS

Many divorced parents of preschool-aged children opt to do pickups and drop-offs at their children's school. For example, one parent drops their preschooler off at school and the other parent picks them up when school is over. This works well because it limits the number of transitions your preschooler has to make. The only time this can become cumbersome is if your preschooler is taking more than one special item back and forth between the homes. Your preschooler will have a backpack and a lunchbox with them, and that's about all a preschooler can carry. If they also need to pack clothing, it will make it much more difficult for them to carry all of this to their classroom. Again, keep clothing at both houses.

While this schedule is convenient, it can be confusing for preschoolers. Make sure you're clear about who is dropping them off and who is picking them up. In some cases, you may want to share this information with the classroom teacher or the school's front office.

Attending preschool is a big change for little ones. Their stress level may increase if a different parent is doing the pickup one or more times per week. Preschoolers do much better when they know what's going to happen. Having a simple calendar in both homes can help preschoolers better understand how long they are with one parent, when they will be going to the next parent's home, and who is dropping off and who is picking up that day. While flexibility is needed in co-parenting and events happen that can disrupt a schedule, be as consistent as you can to prevent your preschooler from feeling additional stress.

Preschoolers should be a part of everyday activities in the home. Preschool-aged children can handle picking up their toys, putting their clothes away, sweeping (or vacuuming if the vacuum is manageable), pouring and stirring in the kitchen, rinsing dishes, and putting some dishes away. When preschoolers get to school, teachers will hand out chores, as well, but the teachers won't call them chores. Some teachers call them helping hands; others call them jobs. It's helpful to use the same term they use at school. Many preschoolers may even get upset if they're not called to help with certain chores, simply because they don't see it as a chore; they see it as a way to help out. Though it may actually be easier to do a chore on your own, allowing your preschooler to be your helping hand increases their self-esteem, makes them feel an active part of the house, and teaches them responsibility.

Preschoolers have a social life! This social life comes in the form of school and playdates. Some parents have enrolled their children in extracurricular activities at this point. Know that your support and involvement in the activity helps your children feel more at home with you. For example, if your preschooler wants to participate in four-year-old T-ball, but only one parent is taking them to T-ball, it makes this part of the divorce harder on them. They've lost a parent in the home and are now losing one in the stands. Yes, your time with your preschooler is already limited, and it can feel like outside activities take more time away, but they only get one chance at childhood. Support them by chauffeuring them to these activities and attending them. Your preschooler will be thrilled you are there.

YOUNG CHILDREN

With this age group, most of the pickups and drop-offs likely happen at school. The children in this age group have a firmer grasp on where they're going, but calendars in both homes are still helpful. If, during the school day, your children are wondering whether they have to get on the bus or wait by the carpool lane or who's picking them up, they aren't concentrating on their lessons, so be sure they are clear about this before leaving for school.

If a special item is going back and forth, it should be able to fit in their backpack. Remember, their lives are all about their peers right now and they just want to fit in. Anything that makes them stand out, like having to carry extra bags to school, can add pressure to their day.

Children of any age may say they don't want to go to their other parent's house, and they do so for several reasons. Some children say this because they believe it's what the parent wants to hear. Sometimes it's because the rules at the other parent's house are different, and in other situations, it may be that they don't feel like their parent is present while they're there. If you hear this from your children, make an effort to understand the reason behind it and empower your children by suggesting they talk through the situation with your co-parent.

A great example of this is the story of Molly. Molly told her dad she didn't want to go to her mom's house, which worried Molly's dad. His divorce with Molly's mom was not amicable, and while they were starting to co-parent, they still had a long way to go. Rather than badmouthing Molly's mom, he sat down with Molly and said, "You and Mom have always had so much fun together. Why don't you want to go?"

Molly told her dad that when she went to her mom's house, her mom was always busy. When her mom got home from work, she would make dinner and then she would clean up the kitchen. After that, there was just a little bit of time until Molly had to go to bed. Molly said her mom would spend this time at her computer. In other words, Molly felt that even though she was at her mom's house, she wasn't getting to spend any time with her. She also told her dad that it made her upset to see her mom crying so often.

Molly's dad told her she should try to talk to her mom about this. He explained that her mom couldn't do anything to change the situation if she didn't know it was upsetting Molly. So Molly went to her mom's house and talked about how she felt. Molly excitedly returned to her dad's home and told him that she and her mom had cooked dinner together and would make it a routine. She also said that her mom thought it would be a good idea to read books with her before bed instead of using her computer. In this situation, it wasn't that Molly didn't want to go to her mom's; she simply wanted to feel like a part of her mom's home. Molly was thrilled to take on a little extra work (like cooking dinner), knowing it meant she was getting to spend time with her mom. This also helped Molly feel like she was a participant in her mom's household, not just a guest.

Chores get a bad rap, but they don't always have to be cumbersome. Children in this age group can take on just about any chore, but know that some will require supervision (for example, using chemicals or sharp objects like knives). That supervision is a wonderful time to bond. Make a game of the chores that have to get done and work together!

Young children are building a social circle. They are getting involved in various extracurriculars and expanding their lives to include more than school and their homes. Playdates and sleepovers will become a regular part of your life as a parent of young children. The hard part of this expanded lifestyle means your one-on-one time with your children will be cut short as you drive to and from practice, take them to and from birthday parties and sleepovers, and attend games and tournaments. It's part of life at this age, and it's all wonderful for your children to experience. Schedule dinners together whenever possible and spend a few extra minutes in conversation with your children when you can (car rides are a great opportunity for this). It will keep your relationship strong and the lines of communication open as they grow.

PRETEENS

Your preteens will learn the ropes of pickup and drop-off pretty quickly. The need for long good-byes lessens simply because of their age. Many parents have told me that they feel like their preteen is happy to get rid of them when they go to their other parent's house! Parents of preteens have to work hard to stay engaged with their children.

Many of the handoffs will happen at school. Logistically speaking, it's the easiest way to handle it, but when school is not in session, this is a great opportunity to work with your preteen on responsibility. While parents are involved in packing what their younger children may need to take back and forth, this can be a preteen's responsibility. At this age, many children have phones or tablets, and while it's hard to imagine a preteen forgetting their phone, it's not so difficult to imagine a preteen forgetting their charger for it. If you and your co-parent do not have dual chargers or electronics at each house, this is a chance to help your preteen make a list of what needs to go back and forth and check it off before they leave. Backpacks, homework, library books, chargers, and electronics are a few of the items that come to mind. Communicate the list to your co-parent so they can do the same thing.

Transitions aren't as difficult for preteens as it is for their younger counterparts, but transition time is still needed. Even if you and your co-parent have consistent routines and expectations between the homes, each home feels different and your preteen's role in each house is different. Give your children time to change their mind-set from what works for them at your co-parent's house to what works at yours. Many preteens just want to spend an hour or two in their bedroom when they get to the other home, and then they want to spend time with their parent. While you may have been counting down the hours to see your preteen again, they have spent that time getting ready for the transition by reviewing their list so nothing's forgotten and packing. Giving them a little space is a great way to allow them to settle in before family time.

Your preteen can take on any chore in the house. In my home, my favorite way to communicate the need for chores is saying that because everyone lives in the house, everyone is responsible for it . . . but everyone is responsible for something different. Everyone in my family participates in "chore day." We list the chores on slips of paper, put them in a hat, and everyone picks a task. We throw on some great music and get to work! Within an hour or two, the house is sparkling, and everyone has had as much fun as possible while participating. When preteens, as well as teenagers, see everyone participating, they become more engaged in the activity. They don't feel like "the help" and learn the value of accomplishment that comes with helping out around the house.

The social life of a preteen is hard to keep up with! School events, sports and clubs, and time with friends can make any parent feel like a chauffeur. When you're a divorced parent, you can feel like you don't get enough time with your preteen, and one-on-one time is very important. The key to ensuring you get adequate time to simply enjoy being with your preteen is careful planning and scheduling.

I worked with a divorced mom, Sarah, with two sons, ages 11 and 13. The boys started telling their mom they didn't want to go to their dad's house anymore. When she dug deeper, she learned that their dad, Jeff, didn't let them go to any friends' houses on the weekends they spent with him. I suggested that Sarah open up to Jeff to understand if this is true, and if so, why. I also helped her see the situation from his perspective so she could speak to him with empathy.

When Sarah spoke to Jeff, he expressed that this was his time with the boys, and he didn't want to give his time up for people the boys were with all week at school. He wanted to go fishing and hiking with them. Sarah understood his point of view, but also her sons' perspectives. She communicated that the boys were feeling like their thoughts about how to spend time at Jeff's home didn't matter, and this made them not want to go. She helped Jeff consider their points of view and offered to help him come up with a balance between his time with the boys and the boys' time with their friends. Soon, Jeff began hosting gaming parties with his sons' friends Friday night into Saturday on some weekends, but spent Sundays fishing or hiking with the boys. They were able to find the best of both worlds, but most important, the boys felt heard by their dad.

Sarah and Jeff were able to have this discussion because they had committed to a positive, child-focused co-parenting relationship. Sarah and I knew that Jeff wouldn't take this as an attack and would make any necessary changes. Not every co-parenting relationship is like that. Some co-parents empower their children by suggesting they have a discussion with their other parent. In this case, it would have been acceptable for Sarah to have talked to her boys about positive ways to bring this up with their dad.

Your preteens' social life is very important and should be fostered, but it does mean spending less time with your children. Some families find that blocking certain evenings or weekend days help keep everyone together—even if it's only one evening a week. For example, if you make every Sunday evening a family dinner night and communicate that routine to your children, it gives them plenty of time to plan other activities, but keeps you all at the table on Sunday. This shows your preteens that you are still a family; it just looks different now.

TEENAGERS

When it comes to transition day with teenagers, like with most school-aged children, the majority of it happens at school. You may drop your teenager off at school, and after school, they may hop on the bus to head to their other home. Though a parenting plan should be in place listing the placement schedule, many parents of teenagers find there is more flexibility with this age group. Do continue to keep a placement schedule; the consistency will help your teenager's life feel more stable. But flexibility is also important, so take into account your teenager's level of independence.

Despite their age and maturity, teenagers still need transition time when arriving at the other home. Teenagers are much more able to communicate the differences between the homes than younger children. One teenager told me that his mom's house is filled with laughter and is in constant movement, while his dad's house is more "chill" and feels relaxing. For him, neither home is better than the other. Both parents worked to keep the rules and expectations the same, but each house felt different to him. He spent the first hour in his room adjusting to a different lifestyle each time he transitioned.

Many parents feel like giving their teenager chores takes away from the already little time they have with their kids, but working chores into everyday routines actually prevents that from happening and makes your children feel like active participants in the home. Give them a list of chores to accomplish when they're at home with you and ask if they'd like to discuss ideas for working those chores into their schedule.

Keep in mind, though, that the schedule teenagers are expected to keep can be a hindrance to getting chores done. They're in school early in the morning and participate in classes that require their full attention all day long. If they have an after-school job or are participating in sports, they go from a full day of mental work directly to a few hours of physical work. From there, they come home to complete possibly hours of homework. Teenagers are not given enough credit for all they do in a day! With that said, their busy schedule doesn't make you their maid or butler. Asking them to take out trash and sweep floors is reasonable; these are jobs that take maybe 15 minutes. If they aren't active participants in making the house run, it's much harder for your home to feel like theirs.

Teenagers are fairly independent. They're making plans throughout the week with their friends, and many teenagers are executing these plans on their own because they're driving. It's important to let them live their lives—within reason. They're still your children, and you still need to establish your expectations. I recommend that co-parents have a similar curfew for their teenagers, and I urge you to have a serious talk with your teenagers about driving under the influence and getting in a car with a driver who has been using drugs or alcohol.

All teenagers will be exposed to drinking and drugs, and many teenagers will want a way out of dangerous or uncomfortable situations without looking like they don't fit in. A great idea is to create a code word with your teenager. If they text you this code word, you'll reply immediately with an excuse for them to leave a party or gathering. Then, you will go pick them up. This reduces the chances they will get in a car with someone who may be under the influence of alcohol or drugs. Communicate this information to your co-parent, or better yet, have a conversation as co-parents so your teenager has both of you on board to ensure their safety. In cases like this, it doesn't matter whose day it is; it matters that your children are safe.

Besides friendships, dating is a part of many teenagers' lives. With only one parent in a home, there's more potential for your teenager to find time alone with their significant other. This is one of those parental decisions you should make together when you create your parenting plan. Are you teaching abstinence? Are you teaching safe sex? Do bedroom doors need to remain open? How much alone time is okay? Is it okay to have their girlfriend or boyfriend at the house if you aren't home? These rules should be consistent at both homes.

What if your teenager watches movies in the basement with their significant other at your co-parent's house, but you require them to watch movies in the family room? With this comparison, they may feel that you don't trust them, which makes it harder for them to open up with you. That doesn't mean you should compromise on your values or your rules; it simply mean that you should have a conversation about trust. Trust is the most important thing to a teenager. They want to know you trust them and if they do make a mistake, you'll teach them how to regain your trust. Parenting teenagers is not for the faint of heart. Doing so from two different homes requires constant communication, trust, benefit of the doubt, and patience.

YOUNG ADULTS

Unlike younger children, there are no handoffs with your young adult. There may not even be a schedule for parenting time. If they're coming home for a break, talk to them about what works for them. Perhaps they can spend part of the time at your house and part of the time at your co-parent's house. Work with your co-parent on scheduling time with your children, too, but respect what your children choose to do. Splitting time between your co-parent's home and yours seems to make the most sense, but young adults don't come home just to see their parents. They come home to see their friends, too.

Many young adults report feeling angry at one of the parents after a divorce. They view the divorce through the eyes of the experiences they've had. That limited experience can lead to judgments that feel unfair. Because of their age, the way to heal the relationship is to respect their opinions and give them space. It's also important to offer to spend time together to have a conversation about their feelings and perspectives or anything else they want to discuss.

The key to making your young adult feel at home where you live is to plan to spend time with them there. Also, young adults who are staying at home for any length of time should be part of household chores, like cooking dinner together and cleaning the kitchen afterward.

This is a great time in parenting. Your children are off exploring life somewhat on their own. They still need you, but not like they did when they were younger. At this point, many parents and young adults start to take on a sort of friendship. Meaningful conversation starts to define time together rather than homework, sports, or driving them around.

Navigating Loss

Now that they are transitioning from one home to another fairly regularly (hopefully with your parenting plan in place), your children are realizing that the divorce is for real (though many children hold out hope for reconciliation). As life begins to move on and they're settling into life in two homes, reality sets in, and many parents start to see regression, anger, or changes in behavior at this point. In this section, I'll give you some red flags to watch out for and some ideas to help your children cope with the reality of your new lives together.

During this time, it's important to work on your own healing, too. It's difficult for parents to see their children hurting, and it's even more difficult when parents feel like it's their fault. Your own emotions will be triggered as you work with your children. In fact, the majority of the parents I work with report that, at this stage, they thought divorce would look a lot different than it does and they feel just as lost as they did at the beginning of it. They experience a combination of anger, loneliness, excitement, and insecurity.

As you read this section, the focus is on your children and their emotional well-being, but you can't fully be there for them if you aren't working on your own emotional healing, as well. Revisit the tools in chapter 1 and use them at this time.

TOUGH QUESTIONS, COMPASSIONATE ANSWERS

This stage of the divorce process comes with its own common questions from your children. Regardless of age, remember they may not always be looking for the answers; rather, they're looking for assurance that this won't happen to them. Here are two versions of the most common questions I hear and inspiration to help you come up with the answer:

Question: Why does Mom cry all the time?

Answer: *I'm sorry to hear she's crying a lot. That must make you sad to see. Did you know that it's okay to cry? I don't know why Mom is crying, but I do know that if you told her it made you sad because you want her to be happy, she would love that. You make both Mom and me happy. Do you want to talk to her alone or do you want me there?*

Note: if you are in a high-conflict situation, this is an opportunity for empathy, and it will likely make things worse to have you there.

Question: Dad's apartment is so small. Why can't we let him live here?

This question comes in many forms, and it's showing empathy on your children's part. Some families separate and are able to maintain similar lifestyles, whereas others cannot. Children generally want to see fairness, so it may be confusing to them if they notice a difference in lifestyles.

Answer: *I know it's very difficult to live in two homes, especially when one looks different from the other. I know Dad is doing everything he can to make sure it feels like home for you. The size of the home isn't as important as the people in it, and Dad's so proud to have you there.*

Toddlers are still building up their vocabulary and aren't able to effectively verbalize any loss they may be feeling. You will need to watch out for changes in behavior, sleep schedules, or difficulty during handoffs. If your toddler is suddenly saying they don't want to go with your co-parent, it doesn't necessarily mean there's something wrong at the other house. Many toddlers are simply trying to communicate that they want their parents together. If they show you they don't want to go with their other parent, in the toddler's mind, their other parent could stay with you. If no one leaves, Mom and Dad are together again.

If you notice any sudden changes in your toddler's behavior during this stage, it will be very important for you and your co-parent to come to an understanding regarding this behavior and how to handle it. Your community may have several parenting experts who can help you manage what you're seeing, or you can look for Love and Logic and Triple P: Positive Parenting Programs online, different types of curriculum to help parents manage any behaviors in their toddlers that they're struggling with (see Resources on page 126). This type of curriculum can help the high-conflict parents because it removes some of the decision-making with regard to how to help their toddler at this time; the online expert will build a plan with you.

The words you use with a toddler are important in building their vocabulary. Use the word *home* when describing your house *and* your co-parent's house. Continue to call your co-parent Mom or Dad when speaking to your toddler. The word *family* meant one home with Mom and Dad living in it, but now it means two homes, where Mom lives in one and Dad lives in the other. SesameStreet.org has excellent videos about divorce and even a workbook to help your toddler through this (see Resources on page 126).

Preschoolers have a bigger vocabulary than toddlers, but they still may not be able to effectively communicate the fears or sadness they're feeling at this stage. They're still getting used to going back and forth between the homes and no longer seeing Mom and Dad together. Some preschoolers show this by asking to talk to their other parent during bedtimes, asking if their other parent can come over for dinner, or showing either excitement or sadness when handoffs happen. Be patient with your preschooler at this time.

Some parents report that their preschooler has said they love their other parent more or that they wish their other parent was there with them. Don't take this personally. It doesn't mean your preschooler doesn't love you. Remember that one of the many emotions they're feeling is anger.

One family I worked with divorced right after their daughter, Sarah, turned four. When Sarah's dad would discipline her or would tell her that it was bedtime, she would cry and say, "I miss Mommy!" Her dad was worried she didn't want to be with him. It broke his heart. When Sarah was with her mom and was told it was time for bed or was disciplined, she would cry and say, "I miss Daddy!" Sarah's mom was heartbroken, as well. She felt like Sarah never wanted to spend time with her. All Sarah was doing was trying to communicate that she wanted Mom and Dad together. She was angry that they weren't together anymore, and that anger came out during difficult emotional times for her, like bedtime and discipline.

When I worked with Sarah's parents, I was able to set up a consistent phone or video chat schedule so Sarah could see that even though her parents lived in different homes, they weren't leaving her. They were simply a phone call away. When Sarah would say, "I miss Mommy/Daddy!" during discipline times, I encouraged her parents to respond lovingly but continue with the consequences for the behavior. It's important to acknowledge your preschooler's feelings, but it's also important to show your preschooler that you can get through it together. It's been years since Sarah's parents divorced. Today, she is a happy, thriving child who loves both her parents. Though there are times when she tells her mom or dad that she misses the other parent, they're able to set up a phone call or video chat, and she moves on.

YOUNG CHILDREN

This age group is growing emotionally. While their younger counterparts may have a smaller range of emotions (for example, happy, sad, and angry), young children's range of emotion grows. Their emotions include frustration, agitation, and jealousy, among many others. Helping your children understand and name what they're feeling helps you teach them how to overcome it. Remember that whatever they're feeling is justified; it's important to understand it, feel it, and move on from it.

You may see some changes in behavior with this age. Many parents report that their children are shutting down emotionally. When they expect a certain emotion from their children, something else is occurring. Consider Andy's case, for example.

Andy's parents divorced when he was in second grade. His dad moved into a new house over winter break. Andy was excited to help his dad move. He felt like his helper and like he was becoming a man like his dad. Andy was a good student, well behaved, and liked by his peers and teachers. His parents checked in with Andy throughout this process, and Andy always seemed fine. By spring break, however, Andy's teachers were noticing a change in him. He was becoming aggressive with his peers whenever he struggled to understand the lessons. He would pound his fists on the ground, throw his pencils, and stopped playing with some of his friends at recess.

The teachers called Andy's surprised parents in. When his parents sat him down to talk about it, Andy shared, in his own words, that he'd been trying to stay upbeat about the divorce because he didn't want his parents to get upset again, but he hated it. His dad's move made it feel real. He hated that they didn't live together anymore. His parents worked with a family therapist to help Andy redefine family, and months later, Andy was back to himself.

Therapists and support groups are some of the available resources to help your children through this stage. "Family" is redefining, and it may take a third party to help your children feel less alone in it. Many times, simply talking to other kids who have gone through the same thing gives children relief. Use the resources you have available to you if you notice something changing. Address issues early. Just as you would take your children to see a doctor if they were physically unwell, take them to see a therapist when they're not feeling emotionally well.

PRETEENS

Many preteens benefit from talking to a counselor. Remember that this age is when they start to show their independence. They're learning what it means to do some things on their own and rely a little less on their parents. They may not want to tell you what they're thinking or feeling because they want to handle the situation on their own. While some preteens may be capable of doing that, having them work with a therapist has more to do with showing your preteen that it's okay to reach out for support than whether or not they can handle it themselves.

If you give some preteens a history book, they can learn what's in it by reading through it, but that doesn't mean they shouldn't have a history teacher. According to a November 2017 *Associated Press* article written by Lindsey Tanner, more preteens are self-harming and the rate of suicide has gone up more over the last 10 years than ever before. Preteens rely on their peers for ideas about how to handle difficult times. Divorce is one of the most difficult things your preteens may go through, so if you feel that your preteen and you do not have a completely open relationship, find a therapist for them, and let the therapist do what they're trained to.

If your preteen is hiding away in their bedroom, is more emotionally reserved than usual, changes their hygiene routine, or adopts a new style of clothing, these are red flags. Again, use the resources in your area, knowing that getting outside help will help your preteen stabilize and continue to grow emotionally.

TEENAGERS

Teenagers handle loss in a lot of different ways. Some teenagers tap into their pain and use it creatively. Think about the teenagers who write songs, produce art, or write. This is a positive way of dealing with emotions. Other teenagers have a strong group of friends to talk to. It's good to get the feelings out with a trusted group. Other teenagers keep it bottled up, however.

They may feel like it's something they can't or shouldn't talk about, or maybe they don't know how to talk about it. Much like with the preteen group, your teenager may suddenly change behaviors related to their hygiene (for example, they will shower less or won't wash their hair), change the way they dress, or their grades may drop.

Depending on the age of your teenager, how often you're checking in with them, and your relationship, you may want to ask your teenager if they'd like to see a counselor. Give them the option, telling them that many people see therapists and that these therapists have to keep what the teenager says confidential. Know that unless your teenager says that they want to harm themselves or someone else, what they say in the counselor's office is between them and the counselor. This is a safe space for them to get everything out and learn new coping skills for dealing with the divorce.

Your child may not be home to truly transition as often as the other ages, so this can be an especially difficult time for both them and you. Remind them of the mental health offerings, either at their college, through their health plan or at free clinics. Today, there is a great emphasis on the mental health of young adults, so many of the services geared toward them are free or very low cost.

If your young adult is in college, know that the staff members on campus are experts in communicating with students who are starting to make the transition away from their parents. The staff can put them in touch with support groups and one-on-one support. If you feel it's necessary, reach out to your young adult's academic advisor; they are usually the lynchpin in your student's college career. Though the advisor likely won't be the one to offer support, they do have the contacts and hopefully a relationship with your student and can guide them on the right path.

Keep communication open with your young adult and remain flexible as they work through their new normal, too. They may try several things out before deciding on what works for them. Don't take any of this personally. Be supportive and appropriately open with your young adult.

Staying Sane about School

School is where your children spend the majority of their time. Your role as parents does not change in the school. You are still there to support their learning and work with the teachers, even if you and your co-parent are not working together. Regardless of the level of conflict between you and your co-parent or the age of your children, here are tips to help you and your children:

1. **Talk to your children's teachers so they can make two copies of communications.** Many schools have a "Mom" folder and a "Dad" folder so that regardless of when communication is handed out or whose parenting day it is, both parents receive the communication. Be respectful of your co-parent's folder and leave the items in there. It only hurts the children when one parent doesn't receive communication. Parents with joint custody both have access to information about their children as well as all communication. If your children's school has an online system for communication, that's even better. Make sure your e-mail is listed and check it often.

2. **Have consistent rules about homework.** If your children are expected to read for 20 minutes every night, make sure you both follow through on it. Allow books to go back and forth. This helps your children learn responsibility. If a book is too valuable to transport in their backpack, a library is another option. Both of you can and should be signing off on any assignment notebooks or reading logs. Consistency between the homes is key here.

3. **Use an app like Artkive or Keepy to take pictures of the artwork your children make.** These are wonderful tools that allow both parents to see and hold on to the many art projects that will come home over the years. It limits fighting over the projects as well as saves space in your home. If both co-parents would like the actual artwork, work together to split what comes through. Once per month, take the artwork you have and give half of it to your co-parent. If they do the

same thing, you both have actual copies of half of it and access to all of it.

4. **Keep on top of your children's progress.** Naturally, one of you will likely be better at reviewing grades and noting missing assignments. Many schools have this information online so parents have easy access to it. Communicate with your co-parent constantly if your children are struggling. The goal here is for your children to get through school successfully. If they're struggling, placing blame isn't helpful; managing the issues is.

5. **Do your best to attend parent-teacher conferences.** While it would be ideal if you and your co-parent can attend these events as a team, the most important thing is that your children know you're there and that you are interested in what's going on with them at school.

6. **From classroom presentations, graduations, and concerts to sports events and field trips, there's a lot going on at your children's school over the year.** Whenever possible, you and your co-parent should make every effort to attend the event. Here are a few further tips:

   • You and your co-parent can alternate accepting opportunities to chaperone field trips.

   • Both parents should have the chance to take pictures with their children after the event, regardless of who your children are going home with that day or evening. Especially if you are the one taking your children home, allow enough time for your co-parent to congratulate your children, exchange hugs, and take pictures. Be respectful of your co-parent's time, as these moments also make the good-byes easier. Your co-parent and your children will appreciate the time together.

- Keep in mind that older children will likely want to chat with their friends and take pictures with them after an event, too. This is an important time for them, so be flexible.

- For events like graduation, it's likely that other family members will be in attendance. Everyone should have a chance for hugs, congratulations, and pictures.

- Graduation from high school and college are the two biggest academic milestones for your children. Both parents should absolutely attend.

- If the event calls for a celebration afterward, the co-parent who doesn't have placement can schedule a celebration for another day, and it will feel just as special to your children.

- It's up to you and your co-parent whether or not you sit together at these events. (However, some daycares automatically put family members together unless they've received a note not to do so.) If possible, sit together at events. If not, know that your children have put in a lot of effort to participate in the event, and they just want you to acknowledge the work they did to get to this point. Your presence is what's most important.

Your children will spend more hours per week in school than they'll spend with you. The best way to support your children throughout the divorce process is to be and remain involved in their school life. Your children benefit most when you and your co-parent are active participants in their academic lives.

Birthdays, Holidays, and Other Celebrations

Kids love to celebrate! That love of celebration doesn't change after divorce, but children of divorce may be more apprehensive about it. At this stage, your children are getting used to living in two homes, and if there is a celebration coming up, you can bet they're worried about it. Who will attend? Whose house will be at? Will their parents argue or ignore each other? Will there be one celebration or two? In the following sections, I give you tips based on their ages to ease their minds so they can focus on what's most important—the celebration! No matter what, this is about your children, not you and your co-parent. Keep the focus on them and remain flexible.

When it comes to holidays, you will ideally have built a holiday schedule into your parenting plan. Perhaps you and your co-parent will spend different holidays with your children on alternate years. For example, if your co-parent has the children for Thanksgiving, perhaps you will have the children that year for another holiday, and then you switch the following year. Find what works for both of you. For example, if you are Christian, this may mean that you'll miss them opening gifts first thing on Christmas morning some years. Other religions have their own but similar traditions, and likewise, you may miss participating in traditional observances on the actual date on alternate years. However, you can still maintain the tradition even if it doesn't happen on the actual day.

When it comes to one time events such as religious milestones and graduations, know that what's most important is that your children feel special. It doesn't matter if they're going home with your co-parent afterward; you can still celebrate their achievements on another day. The most important thing is that both of you are at the special event to support and cheer for your children.

TODDLERS

Toddlers handle changes to the schedule best when they know what to expect. Though celebrations are exciting, they still need to know what's going to happen to enjoy themselves fully. Tell your child who is expected to be at a celebration and what will likely occur. If you and your co-parent have a high-conflict relationship, it's best to keep celebrations separate. If you believe that both you and your co-parent and your friends and family can get along for the sake of your toddler, then it may work to create one celebration for them.

PRESCHOOLERS

Preschoolers love celebrations. An upcoming celebration will keep them filled with anticipation for days! Just like their toddler counterparts, communicate what you can to your preschooler to ease any anxiety they may have about the event. If you are creating one celebration for your preschooler, share the guest list with them only if you are completely sure those people are definitely attending. For example, be absolutely certain that your co-parent is coming to an event before telling your preschooler they will be there. If the co-parent does not show up, it will be very hard for your preschooler to understand.

YOUNG CHILDREN

How celebrations look starts to change a bit with young children. For example, this age group often celebrates birthdays with large parties and invites the entire class. If this is the case and you feel that you and your co-parent are able to get along, it's a great opportunity for both of you to document the fun they have with their friends. If you are not able to attend together, the co-parent who is attending should definitely share photos with the other co-parent. Co-parents can host this party in alternate years so neither one feels left out.

Remember that your preteens are very social. This means that they will want to celebrate their birthday with their friends. While it's important to have family involved, your preteens' focus will be on when they can get together with their peers. Try to compromise with your co-parent, if necessary, to make this possible for your children. When it comes to celebrating with family, will you host a single birthday party or will each family have their own birthday celebration?

Though holidays are generally reserved for family time, your preteens will likely be checking in with their friends on their phones or tablets on the day of the festivities. So, when it's time to celebrate with the family, ask them to put away the electronics so you can be present with each other.

Birthdays for teenagers are more about their friends than they are about you. If your teenager is working and/or involved in many extracurricular activities, planning for their friends to come over may come down to a weekend when nothing is scheduled rather than a weekend with a certain parent.

Many divorced parents find that birthday celebrations with their teenagers are done separately simply because teenagers' lives are so focused on friendships. In the case of one family I worked with, as soon as their daughter turned 14 years old, the large parties with classmates ended, and her parents didn't throw parties together anymore. They celebrated their daughter's birthday separately with a special dinner that included important family members, and their daughter loved it. She had birthday sleepovers with her friends on whatever weekend worked for her. She was able to enjoy time with each of her families and was quick to comment that two celebrations meant two sets of presents!

YOUNG ADULTS

When it comes to smaller events like birthdays for young adults, you can celebrate them whenever it works for you and your children. You and your co-parent can each celebrate separately with your children unless there is a special tradition you've shared for years that you agree to continue. Perhaps you and your co-parent will keep that tradition alive with some tweaks so that it can be celebrated separately.

The holiday schedule is more flexible with young adults. Perhaps they will split the holiday between their parents. For example, maybe they will have Thanksgiving lunch with one family and Thanksgiving dinner with another. Or maybe they will alternate holidays between parents. Your young adult probably has thoughts about what they would like to do, so check in with them.

Aside from graduation, the most significant events you'll have with your young adult are engagement parties and weddings. Obviously these are events neither parent should miss. Speak to your children about how you and your co-parent can make them feel comfortable.

FAMILY RITUALS

From the winter holidays to birthdays to other celebrations, families build tradition. Just because you are
divorced doesn't mean that tradition has to stop. If you
are on great terms with your co-parent, many traditions
can continue as is. You will simply have to decide whose
house hosts that tradition. If you are not on great terms,
you can tweak traditions to keep the feelings associated with them alive in your home.

Traditions are all about the feelings involved. For
example, if you have maintained a tradition to listen to
Christmas music and drink hot chocolate whenever you
put Christmas decorations up, you can continue that
tradition at your home.

In some cases, you will not be involved in the tradition at the same time you would have before the
divorce. Perhaps you have always gone trick-or-treating with your children on Halloween. Your parenting
plan will likely split Halloween between you and your
co-parent. That doesn't mean the tradition ends, however. You and your co-parent might decide to alternate
years, continuing the tradition for your kids. You can
also check if your community has a Halloween party or
a special trick-or-treat event on a day or evening other
than Halloween so you can still help your children dress
up and celebrate with them. Or maybe you want to host
a Halloween party yourself if you can't be a part of the
trick-or-treating fun. Be creative!

If you cannot be there for certain times, like Christmas morning or candle lighting, be supportive and keep
in mind that this is about your children. The last thing
your children want is to feel guilty about enjoying their
time with their other parent. You can still participate in
your traditions with your children, even if it's not at the
exact time you used to do them.

Many divorced families end up creating new traditions naturally as time goes on. Embrace this, knowing that any tradition you share with your children will become part of their childhood memories, and traditions make for feel-good memories.

Discipline Dos and Don'ts

One of the many ways to help your children feel safe is keeping them accountable for what they do. Though no child will willingly line up for grounding or removal of screen time, if they aren't disciplined, they will feel a sense of insecurity.

Regardless of how old their children are, many parents feel like they need to overcompensate for the divorce. They ease up on rules and expectations and don't feel like they need to follow through on consequences. Please understand that the security that comes with a consistent set of rules and consequences is irreplaceable. It would be like your children returning to school after winter break only to discover that the rules they'd been following had changed because the teacher feels bad for them. There would be chaos, and their ability to learn would suffer. The same applies at home. Here are a few rules for co-parents to follow no matter the age of their children:

- Wherever possible, decide together on what the rules and expectations should be. If you cannot decide, work with a parenting expert in your community to help you come up with this part of the parenting plan. While you work with them, decide on the consequences you will both follow through on. Then comes the important part: both parents need to follow through. This should be part of your parenting plan, but if it's not, it's never too late to add it.

- Communicate what is happening with your children to your co-parent. Your co-parent can't back you up and present a united front if they don't know what's happening.

- Keep your cool as much as possible. Sometimes parents need to put *themselves* in a timeout when misbehavior rears its head. If you discipline in anger, your co-parent would have to follow your lead to present a united front and vice versa. It's easier to continue the united front if you both recognize frustration and take a mental break before disciplining.

- Be consistent! If you expect your co-parent to follow your lead, you need to follow theirs. Your children will know where the crack is if one of you does not follow through, and they'll use that to get out of the consequences. It makes your co-parent's life hard and ensures your children never have to listen to the rules.

- When you have a high-conflict relationship or you cannot agree on disciplining, using a phrase like, "I know your mom/dad doesn't do this, but I do" can help you remain an authority figure in your children's eyes even if you are not on the same page with your co-parent. Your consequences can carry over even if your children leave for time with their other parent. Be clear and tell your children, "You have lost an hour of screen time for the next five days you are with me."

Remember that along with new ways to discipline, you are building new routines at this point in your divorce. Some of those routines will become traditions your children will cherish for years. And though a lot in their lives has changed, not everything has to. You will continue to be there for them for the important times and will continue to celebrate their achievements and special events. Support and encourage involvement from your co-parent in whatever way works for your family. Your children simply want to know they are special in the eyes of both of their parents.

Chapter Four

Navigating the
Post-Divorce World

At this point, you are well into life after divorce. New routines have been built, your children have transitioned to life living in two homes, and you're moving on with your life. Part of moving on might mean new relationships and the potential for stepparents. In this chapter, I discuss the best ways to introduce the new person in your life to your children, how to blend families together, and how to keep extended family involved in your children's lives.

New Relationships

We are wired for togetherness. That means that you and your co-parent will likely find yourselves in new relationships at some point. While this is exciting (and scary!) for you, it can be very confusing for your children. They'll worry about their other parent and be fearful of how your role in their life may change. Introductions are just part of the deal when you start dating again. Creating rules for sleepovers and the other adult parts of the relationship serves two purposes: it will help your children understand expectations in their own relationships, and it will ease the transition of your romantic involvement with someone new.

When it comes to dating, it's ideal to save your dates for days and nights when your children aren't with you. Since your time with your kids is already limited, getting a babysitter for them may make them feel as though you don't have time for them. If you are dating someone who has a different schedule than you do, it may sometimes be necessary to get a babysitter, but I recommend being creative with your time together before turning to babysitters. Can you find time for lunch dates? Are you able to meet for an hour or two between times with your children? Can you video chat after the kids are in bed? Some adults will even watch a movie "together" while video chatting from different homes.

Once you've introduced your children to this person, they will be spending more and more time at your house. In general, I advise parents that their new partner should only sleep over if they are okay with their own children having sleepovers when they are in relationships. It's hard to teach abstinence until marriage if you are not following the same rule, so be clear on the rules you want to establish for your children. If you do have sleepovers when your kids are home, consider the questions that may arise and whether or not you would have an honest answer for them.

In the following sections, I'll discuss how to handle introductions with your children depending on their age. Regardless of age, introductions should wait until you are in a relationship that's significant enough to lead to marriage. Remember, the person you introduce to your children as your significant other will become a significant part of their lives, too. If you break up, your children lose that person, too. This person has an influence on your children—good and bad. You are no longer deciding to be in a relationship based on how you feel when you're with someone; you are also making the decision based on the type of person they will be with your children.

Many parents ask how long they should be dating someone before they make the introductions. I don't believe there is a magic number, but you should absolutely be in a serious relationship. A serious relationship will have passed the initial excitement phase, dealt with conflict in some way, and included serious discussions about the future and whether or not you envision a similar version. Before that, it may feel serious, but your relationship has some bridges to pass yet.

Waiting to introduce your children to this person until you're serious prevents them from watching people come in and out of your life and prevents you from having to answer questions about who you've been dating and how long. The only exception to this is with your young adult, which I will discuss shortly.

The last piece to remember is that you are only able to follow these rules yourself. Your co-parent has a different perspective on this and may introduce your children to people before you believe the time is right. The best way to handle this is to remain positive and make the best of the situation for the sake of your children.

Before any introductions take place, give your co-parent a heads-up. You certainly wouldn't want this news sprung on you, and neither would your co-parent. It's awkward to talk about, but necessary if you're getting serious with someone. In ideal situations, your co-parent should get to meet them first. This makes the transition easier on your children when they meet your new partner. It's almost as if your kids are given the okay to like this new person.

Take introductions slow. Start small, like going out for ice cream together and slowly increase your children's time with your new partner. Think of it as steps your partner takes toward being a part of your children's lives. Work up to a fun event like a zoo outing or a baseball game and finally with dinner at your house. Your children are much more likely to embrace this new person if they feel comfortable with them. If they don't have time to process and accept your new relationship, they won't feel comfortable with this person or their role in your life.

TODDLERS

Generally speaking, toddlers fall into one of two categories: they accept new people willingly or are apprehensive of new people. You know your toddler better than anyone, so consider their tendencies as you plan for the introduction. Start small and use phrases like "This is Mom's new friend," or "This is Dad's new friend," when introducing them. Stick to first names for introductions, and let your toddler have fun with the new person.

Keep displays of affection with your new partner at bay in front of your toddler until later on in the introduction stage. If it's too soon, your toddler will be confused. Remember, toddlers are still learning, so if they see that Mommy kisses her new friend on the mouth, they may think it's okay to kiss *their* friends on the mouth. Until you get to the point of calling this person your boyfriend or girlfriend, affection should be neutral. When your toddler becomes used to this person and they've been able to spend time with them in your home, you can talk about what it means to have a boyfriend or girlfriend.

PRESCHOOLERS

Now that they're in school, your preschoolers are getting used to many new people in their lives. You and your co-parent are their constants, so seeing you with someone new may be difficult for them. They're willing to meet this new person, but they may be less willing to accept them as a new member of the family. Keep this in mind as you work through the introduction process.

When it comes to showing your new partner affection, preschoolers are generally grossed out by this. However, they may be more upset by it if they're struggling to get used to the relationship. Take your preschool-viewed affection slowly. Start by holding hands, work up to hugging, and then to kissing over a reasonable amount of time.

Using phrases like those suggested for toddlers ("my new friend") helps keep your new partner's role in your life neutral, allowing your preschooler to get used to their being around more often. Your preschooler may take time to fully warm up to this person. Let them go at their pace. Remember that because you are serious about this person, they'll be around for a while, so it's okay to take things slow if you need to. At some point, you can share that this person is your new boyfriend or girlfriend and what that means.

YOUNG CHILDREN

This age group is smart. You will likely introduce this person as your friend, but they have some thoughts in the back of their mind about what type of friend this person is. Their peers may have stepparents, and they've probably heard stories of their friends' parents dating. Your children may ask you if you "like like" this person or if they're your boyfriend or girlfriend, so be prepared with your answer.

Your children may decide early on that they don't like this person simply because they don't want to lose their role in your life. You are farther along in the divorce process now, and your children have had you all to themselves for a good period of time. Having to share you is a reality many children don't want to face. If they tell you they don't like this person, you'll need to have a conversation with your children. Sometimes personalities clash, and, if that's the case, my advice to you is to find any common ground and build on it. Agree to disagree and respect each other while trying to learn from each other, too.

Keep the lines of communication open, and let your children come to you to discuss what's on their minds. After several meetings with your partner, if your children haven't mentioned anything to you about them, you may want to casually bring this person up. For example, you can say something like, "Do you think we should invite [name] to that?" This keeps it casual, lets your children know you think about that person, and lets you watch them for reactions without your new partner present.

The amount of affection you show with your new partner in front of your young children depends on how well they're handling the relationship. While it's always good to take this part of the relationship slow in front of the children, how slow you take it depends on them. You want your children to feel comfortable with this person, which means you must be sensitive to how your children feel when you're all together.

PRETEENS

Preteens are smart, too. They know if they're being introduced to someone new that this is a romantic partner. Introductions are a little trickier at this age. I advise parents to be open about who this person is and that you've been seeing him or her "for a little while."

Many preteens ask why they didn't know you were seeing someone, and it's a good question. The easiest way to answer this is to let your preteen know that you are telling them about it now because there is something to tell. You can let them know that prior to this, you had gone on some dates with this person, but there wasn't really anything to tell until it got serious. Again, you are the example for your preteen, as they will be entering their own dating years in the near future. They're watching you and may follow your lead in the years to come.

Because your preteens will know that this is someone you're dating, you can start with a dinner. Preteens don't always quickly open up to new people. Many parents take this personally or worry that their preteens don't like their new partner. Give it time. Let them develop a relationship with each other. Just as it's taken you time to develop your relationship, it will take your children time, too.

Your preteen is likely becoming attracted to others, as well. They're learning what it means to be in a relationship by watching other people interact. That includes you and your new partner. Be sensitive to how they're feeling about the relationship, and use that as an initial gauge to decide what level of affection to show in front of your preteen, but then know that what you show is what they will learn from. Would you be comfortable with them engaging in the same type of affection with the people they date when it comes to that time? If not, then that's the type of affection that may need to stay behind closed doors.

TEENAGERS

Many parents tell their teenagers when they've started dating, but that doesn't mean they go into detail about it. Many times, this conversation comes up when a teenager asks point-blank if the parent is dating. It's natural for them to think along these lines. Be appropriately honest. Simple answers like, "Yes, I'm dating," or "No, I'm not dating anyone right now," let your teenagers know that you're okay talking about this subject. It's a good sign if they ask more questions. If your teenagers feel open enough to talk to you about dating, embrace the communication! A general conversation is a great step toward keeping the lines of communication open. Remember, teenagers don't need to know the specifics.

When you introduce your new partner, dinner is an easy way for your partner to start getting to know your children and vice versa. Depending on how your children transitioned following the divorce, you may want to have dinner at your house. If you feel they will not be ready for this new person in your life, having dinners and meetings outside your home will be easier on them. Go slow if your teens are having a difficult time. Some teenagers are happy to see their parents dating because it makes their parents happy. While it will always be "weird" to teenagers to see their parents as anything more than their mom and dad, they do want you to be happy. Take these meetings at your children's pace, and let them develop a relationship with your partner naturally.

Like preteens, your teenagers are watching and learning from you. That includes how you are behaving in a relationship. Teenagers don't want to think of their parents as people. Be sensitive to how your teens feel about the relationship, but also be sensitive to what they're seeing. A teenager may say, "But you're doing it!" when you talk to them about sex and dating. You have a couple of options here. Some parents will say that they themselves are responsible and turn the conversation into a discussion about responsibility. Other parents will explain that there are different rules for teenagers and adults. Whatever you decide, remember that you are their role model.

YOUNG ADULTS

Many parents find themselves transitioning into more of a friendship with their young adults, so while they may not see you dating because they're no longer at home, you may want to talk about it with them during video chats or phone calls. If you feel your young adult is ready to learn you've begun dating, keep the conversation appropriately open with them. Introductions will be easier because they will have heard some good stories about your new partner, will have noticed that you are happy and excited, and may look forward to meeting them.

If your young adult has not handled the divorce well, it's still important to talk to them about dating as more of a heads-up. Talk to your children and tell them that you know this divorce has been hard on them, but you are starting to get back out there and want them to hear it from you. Ask them what they're comfortable hearing about your new significant other, and take things at their pace.

When it comes to introductions, this should be an exciting time. Let your children know you want to introduce them to the person you have been seeing. Make the meeting casual and limit the number of people present. Let your children take things at their own pace with the new relationship.

Young adults are living their own lives; some of it is outside the home, perhaps on a college campus. The rules for sleepovers when your children are home may bend slightly with this age group, depending on your values and morals. If you want to teach abstinence before marriage, you need to show them you are willing to do the same. If you are open to sex before marriage, know that you are setting an example of what that looks like. I do not believe this part of your relationship should be flaunted in front of any children, regardless of age, but many parents are more open about it when their children are older.

TOUGH QUESTIONS, COMPASSIONATE ANSWERS

You are through the transition stage at this point. Your children are well into their new routines, and you're getting to the point of introducing them to new partners. Here are a few of the common questions I hear from families at this point in the divorce process and some inspiration to help you answer them. Remember, sometimes the questions your children are asking aren't really what they want the answer to; they may be using these questions as a gauge to see where things are headed.

Question: I met Mom/Dad's new boyfriend/girlfriend last weekend.

This isn't actually a question; it's a statement usually meant to check your reaction. In ideal situations, you and your co-parent will have discussed this meeting beforehand so this will not be news to you. In this case, choose a response like answer "A." However, if this is news to you, be careful about your response. You may have to conceal any shock or frustration; choose a neutral response like answer "B."

Answer A: *Yes, your Mom/Dad told me. That's exciting! It sounds like you guys had some fun plans, too!*

Answer B: *Oh, that's exciting! Did you do anything fun?*

In either case, refrain from asking your children if they like this new person. It will be tempting, but this information will come out eventually. If you ask your children if they like this person, they may tell you, "They're okay, I guess," simply to protect your feelings.

Question: Why do you [or the other parent] have to date?

For many kids, this is your child's way of asking why they aren't enough to keep you company. Now that you've been divorced for a while, your children have been your company when they're with you. By dating, you're adding another person to the mix, and they want to know where they stand. They may be a little hurt by it, too.

Answer: *Most grown-ups are in relationships, just like Mom/ Dad and I were. It didn't work out for Mom/Dad and me, but that doesn't mean it won't work out for us and someone else. Are you worried that I won't have time with you if I'm [or the other parent is] dating?*

Having one-on-one time with your children will be even more important after your new partner has become a part of your lives, so I'll revisit this later.

New Families

Whether or not your partner has children of their own, you are working at blending families when you bring them into your lives. Your new partner is not going be your children's parent, but they are certainly going to have a parental role. When you think about adding a new partner and any children that come with your new partner, remember that you're adding more people to your children's family.

I like to think about this in much the same way you've been moving through the divorce process so far. It's good news for you, but your children still have to process it and transition through it. Are you telling your children that your partner is moving in? Are you all moving out and into your partner's home? Are you getting married?

When you get serious and start thinking about marriage, many children wonder what they should call their new stepparents. This is a personal choice and should be made by your children. Some children come up with a version of Mom or Dad rather than the person's first name, like Momma Karen rather than Mom. Other children stick with the first name, and that's okay, too. The point here is to make sure your children are the ones to decide what they will call your new spouse and that no matter what they choose, it's acceptable to you as long as it's respectful. The same goes for what they call your co-parent's new partner.

Start with a plan. Work with your new partner about what parenting looks like, how you'll handle discipline, where everyone will sleep, and what your day-to-day schedule will look like. When you have this information prepared, you are better able to answer your children's questions.

To blend the families into one home, someone will have to move. Who will be moving? What do pickups and drop-offs look like now? Will your kids have to get on a different bus? Are they going from having their own room to sharing a room? In areas where you can be flexible, tell your children the plan and let them know you're open to discussion. For instance, if your new partner is moving in with their own kids, maybe your children can discuss how the bedrooms will be set up. Of course, before this discussion comes up, your kids and your new partner's kids will have spent time together. You'll be able to see where natural friendships have developed.

This blending of families can be exciting for your children, but also a little scary. They may wonder if your new marriage will end in divorce, too. They may be worried they will never have you to themselves again. These are natural fears. Consider all of this when you share the news about moving in together. If you think your children will have a hard time accepting this, tell them without your partner present. They will feel more comfortable talking to just you. But if you think they will be happy about the news, you and your new partner can tell them together. Here's some inspiration for what to say:

"You know [name] and I have been dating for a while. Things have been going really well, and we're ready to take our relationship to the next level. [Name] is going to move in here. We're talking about the move happening next month, but I wanted ideas from you about how to help welcome [name] into our home."

Once you've communicated the news to your children, watch for changes in behavior. Sudden changes may indicate that they're worried, and you may need to take them aside for a discussion. You may want to say something like, "I've noticed you haven't been sleeping well lately and that it's been like this since we've talked about [name] moving in. Is there something you're worried about?" Allow your children to express whatever is on their mind so that you can address their concerns.

CREATE A PLAN

Whether one or more people have moved in with you and your children (or vice versa), set the expectations for everyone in the home. Create a "house rules" list. Place a large calendar with schedules in a main area of your home. Keep up with family mealtimes, especially as your family grows. Just as you were very open about the changes that came when you divorced, be open and clear about the changes coming up.

When you build the calendar, build in one-on-one time for you and your children to spend together. Yes, this is a new family unit, but your children will transition better by having individual time with you like they had prior to this change. The same goes for your partner and their children. Though it sounds counterproductive, it goes a lot further in helping the new family bond when the children don't have to worry about losing their parent in the blended family.

All hands should be on deck for the move. Make sure your children are a part of it, no matter how old they are. Consider how difficult it would be for your children if they left to spend time with your co-parent and everything had been moved by the time they returned home. Moving is a lot of work and it may be harder with little ones around, but they are a part of your family, too, and should be involved in what happens during the move.

Expect difficulties in the beginning. This is another transition for your children, so use the strategies discussed in chapter 2. Get on the floor and play with your younger kids as you talk about how it's going. Take older children out for lunch and discuss the new situation with them. If they're struggling, talk about what you can do to make the best of it.

If your family now includes stepsiblings, expect the same types of behavior between them and your children as you would between siblings of the same parents. There will be moments of joy and laughter, moments of arguments and competition, and moments of togetherness. Sibling rivalry isn't limited to children with the same DNA. In a way, sibling rivalry can be good, but it should be constructive. In other words, competition can help children do their best at a task, but respecting each other is most important.

Some blended families find that the blending process is easy and painless, whereas others struggle to find their rhythm. If you are having difficulty with it, working with a family counselor can uncover the hiccups and build family-focused solutions. There's no shame in seeking the support of a professional. If something in your house wasn't working, you'd find a professional to make the repair. If the people in your home are struggling, involving a professional removes some of the struggle, creates solutions, and teaches coping skills.

LOOK THROUGH YOUR CHILDREN'S EYES

This point is another transition for your children. It may be hard to truly gauge how they're feeling through it. In those cases, look at it from your child's point of view. One of the best ways to do this is to sit down after a typical day in your home and write a story about that day from your children's point of view. For example:

"Johnny woke up at 6:30 a.m. when his mom knocked on his door. He lay in bed for 10 minutes before getting up and coming downstairs for breakfast. Johnny's stepdad was making pancakes and asked Johnny if he wanted bananas or strawberries on his. Johnny's mom and stepdad were talking about the art show at Johnny's school that night. They were deciding who would pick Johnny and his sister up from school and make them dinner."

Keep the story going until "Johnny's" bedtime. When you're finished with the day, go back through and really look at the child in the story. Does he like pancakes? Was his stepdad making them the way Johnny liked them? How could he have been feeling when you were discussing who would pick the kids up? Do you think he felt like a burden or loved? Did he wake up in a new room or in his old room? Was anyone in there with him?

Looking at things from another person's point of view requires taking a step back. When you're writing a narrative of the day, it's not based in feeling; it's based on actual events. This is used in family therapy, especially with older children. Each family member chooses a person and writes about the day from that person's point of view. Once you see things from their eyes, you're in a better place to understand and make the best of it.

Extended Family

When you and/or your co-partner get married to someone new, the circle of people your children call family grows. In addition to their parents and siblings, what they call family now includes stepparents, perhaps stepsiblings, and eventually maybe even half-siblings, among others. Today's blended families all look different. In this section, I'll discuss ways to include everyone your children considers family members in their lives. Your children simply want the chance to love all of you. They certainly don't want to feel like loving everyone and wanting to spend quality time with other family members will make you feel bad.

Grandparents are sometimes the last people thought of after a divorce. In many families, grandparents had sleepovers with their grandkids prior to the divorce. Because divorce changes how much time your children are with you, it's a lot harder to give up even more time with your children even if it's to your parents. Generally speaking, if you're sharing placement with your co-parent, it's easiest for each of you to ensure that your children have meaningful time with your individual parents. While it's hard to give up the time, this is about the kids, and they shouldn't miss out on time with Grandma and Grandpa just because their parents divorced. In fact, this time with Grandma and Grandpa can be a time of relief in a world of change.

Aunts, uncles, and cousins are another part of your children's extended family. It's likely you spent time with your siblings before the divorce, so the cousins got to spend time together by default. Try to keep your children's aunts, uncles, and cousins involved in their life. If you regularly got together before the divorce, try to do the same, even though you now have a new partner. Your children will benefit most if both you and your co-parent continue to involve your respective siblings and their children in your children's lives, even if there's not as much time to do so as before.

A divorce doesn't have to end relationships with family members, but many times it does, and children notice. When this happens and your children ask you something like, "Why don't we go see Auntie Jen anymore?" keep your responses short. You can say something along the lines of, "Auntie Jen is Dad's sister, and I know Dad likes to spend time with her. Maybe you and Dad can call her and schedule a visit." Older children understand that, unfortunately, families split when divorce happens, but younger children don't. In their mind, Mom and Dad couldn't make the marriage work, but everyone else is still in their lives. Encourage your co-parent to maintain relationships with people you aren't in touch with anymore.

Hopefully, your new partner's family wants to be part of your children's lives, too. Your partner's family members will require their own introduction. A meal hosted by that side of the family can make the introduction easier. Your children can see what these new members of their family are like in an environment the new family feels comfortable in.

Decide ahead of time with your partner what your children should call your partner's family members: *Grandma and Grandma? Aunt Karen? Uncle Joe?* Something else? Your partner can check with their family members to see if there's a preference. With older children, you can also ask what their preference might be. Remember, this is about the kids, so make sure they're comfortable using any specific titles. When you are all on the same page, introduce them to your children using these names.

My children call their step-grandparents Grandma and Grandpa. My in-laws took on the role of grandparents as if they had always been grandparents to my kids. I believe these titles are earned by how a new partner's parents treat the children and the relationship that develops. These titles aren't necessarily earned solely through blood.

Of course, schedules are going to be tricky when you start adding new family members into the mix. Creativity may need to go into celebrating holidays and birthdays. Some families I work with get together every two months and celebrate all the birthdays that occurred during those two months. It's a huge celebration during which "Happy Birthday" is a hilarious mash-up of everyone's names before candles are blown out.

When it comes to larger holidays, you may be celebrating before or after the actual holiday. It doesn't always matter when you celebrate, simply that you do. This is more about building traditions and family time than presents and dessert. Keep your expectations realistic and remember that your children are doing the same thing with their other family. For some kids around the holidays, every weekend is another party. This isn't necessarily bad, but it does impact their usual routines, which impacts behavior. Keep in mind that this is temporary, and try to be flexible and patient during these times. Provide your children with as much downtime as you can over the holidays.

Be flexible if your co-parent's family is throwing parties. Remember, these people may not be in your life anymore, but they are still in your children's lives. For example, if your child's closest cousin is having a birthday party on a weekend when your child is with you, can you figure out a way to for your child to attend for your child's sake? It's hard to have your time with your children limited any more than it already is, but an exchange of weekends or another creative way to make it work benefits your children. They shouldn't feel bad about wanting to go to a party even if it means they're missing time with you. In their minds, this isn't about you; it's about them having fun with their cousin. Make an effort to look at the situation through your children's eyes when events like this come up.

Your children are loved by many people. Isn't that a wonderful thing? Too often parents get stuck in feeling like they don't have enough time with their children so they don't want to give any of that precious time up to others. But when you look at it from your children's perspective, you realize that your children simply want to love these people back. Their childhood is going to fly by. Wouldn't it be great if you made sure their childhood had many wonderful memories that included *everyone* who loved them?

They say it takes a village to raise a child, and many times that village is your children's extended family. You can't bring the village in unless you're willing to share the time you have with your children. Yes, it will take creativity and sacrifice, but the memories your kids make will be worth it.

Chapter Five

Strengthening Your Bond

You've built your new routines, your children are through the transition, and you and your co-partner may be in new relationships. Now that your family has been redefined, it's time to focus on strengthening your bond with your children. It doesn't matter if they're young or older—a bond can always be fortified. This chapter revisits your parenting plan, helps you make new decisions for and with your children, and discusses ways to strengthen your relationship after the transition.

Revisit Your Parenting Plan

At this point, quite a bit of time has passed since you've looked at your parenting plan. When it was created, your family may have had a different set of needs than it has now. Many families report that they learned a lot from following the parenting plan in their daily lives. When you write the plan, it's not possible to think of every situation. Sometimes you find that an idea was good when it was put in the plan, but in practice, it didn't work as well as you thought it would. Now is a good time to take a look at what's working and what could be improved on.

Throughout this book, you've read about red flags and learned how to talk to your children throughout the stages of the divorce. When you revisit your parenting plan, keep in mind everything you've learned and talked about with your children. What have you seen your children struggle with, if anything? Has your co-parent noticed the same things? It's a good idea to run through your communication with your co-parent to look for situations where your children were struggling. When you revisit those events, did you find a solution? If so, how can you incorporate those solutions into an updated parenting plan?

Your children will have aged during this process, so while your focus when you first divorced may have been on establishing similar routines between both homes based on the age of your children, perhaps the goal is now to come together on rules for getting and responsibly using a cell phone. Revisit chapter 1 and review the milestones for your children's age group as you take a look at the parenting plan. Consider what you're facing individually as parents and how you want to face that together as co-parents. A united front will always be in your children's best interest, no matter their age.

One couple I worked with separated before their baby was born. They created their parenting plan before their child was born so they could start following it right away. This family used ages and stages as a guide. When their baby was born, she would remain with her mom the majority of the time because she was breastfeeding. Her dad would visit whenever it worked with his co-parent's schedule. This ensured their child and her dad would be able to bond, as well. As soon as the baby finished breastfeeding, she would begin overnight visitation with her dad. The co-parents built a workable schedule so that by the time she was two years old, she would have equal time with both parents. At each stage, they revisited the parenting plan and adjusted it as their child's needs changed to keep the plan child-focused.

Many co-parents come to see that certain areas of the plan are too vague and each parent had a different understanding of it. For instance, a statement like, "The summer schedule will begin the Sunday after the last day of school and will end the Sunday before the first day of the next school year," may leave room for interpretation. Does this mean the normal rotation for weekends remains the same? If so, one parent may have their children for 10 to 12 days in a row. Make a note of issues that come up consistently and work with your co-parent to rewrite the plans so there is less likelihood they will be misinterpreted.

As mentioned earlier, I recommend meeting with your co-parent regularly to discuss the things happening in your children's lives and to ask each other questions regarding the parenting plan. Make a note at these meetings and compile these notes as often as you feel it's necessary to change the parenting plan. Work together to rewrite or add to the parenting plan and have it notarized and placed in your file with the court in which your divorce file resides.

If you and your co-parent aren't able to come to an agreement regarding changes that need to be made, you can use the services of a mediator or a divorce coach. These professionals will sit down with you and your co-parent to discuss your goals and work to guide you both down the path of compromise for the sake of your children. The mediator or coach will ask questions to keep you both child-focused and may even recommend ideas to fit both your children's needs and yours. These professionals charge an hourly fee, but they generally have a lower hourly rate than a lawyer.

If a mediator or divorce coach is not the route you want to take, but you are unable to come to an agreement, you always have the option of retaining a lawyer. The lawyer will ask for your goals and will file a motion to make this change with the court in the county you divorced in. If your co-parent retains a lawyer, they may file a similar motion with your co-parent's goals. When this goes to a judge, that judge may require you to attempt mediation and work toward agreement, but if that mediation is not successful, the judge will decide for you.

These are all options for you when you feel a parenting plan should be revisited and changed. However, if you aren't able to collaborate and compromise on the changes being requested, remember that a judge decides what changes will be made and what they will look like for the parents. Many parents don't realize that when the judge decides for them, they've lost the chance to make the decision together.

Co-parenting is not easy, but if you're able to keep your emotions in check and remember that compromise is necessary, you'll find that making changes to your parenting plan does not have to be difficult. Be flexible and open-minded, knowing that your co-parent may have a different perception than you. Neither one of you is right or wrong. Chances are good that you're both right, and you just see things from different points of view.

How decisions are made is one of the areas in the parenting plan that one or both of the co-parents may feel needs revision or adjustment. Hopefully, you and your co-parent went into your divorce trying to work together. If you didn't, I hope you're getting to that collaborative place now. Whether or not you are collaborating and compromising with your co-parent, decision-making is a pain point for many parents. Have you noticed that you disagree on decisions and hit a stalemate? Do you feel like one of you gives in simply to avoid an argument and this has led to resentment? Does it seem as though no decisions are being made?

If you find yourself in those categories, I recommend working with a divorce coach. This professional will work with you and your co-parent to create some rules of engagement when it comes to decision-making. They'll walk you through the traps they see each of you falling into and how to turn that around for the sake of your children. Some parents put mediation or a divorce coach into their parenting plan as a step they're required to take when major decisions come up. These parents know that a third party can be helpful to cut through any potential conflict and get right to the point.

Decide Now on Decisions Later

When it comes to decision-making, many parents make decisions early on for events that will come up later. If you have young children, you will be making many decisions for them over the years. Some of those decisions, or at least a plan for making those decisions, can be handled now. As you're thinking about your parenting plan, you may have experienced some occasions when decisions should have been made between you and your co-parent but weren't. That experience can help you and your co-parent make decisions later for your children.

Remember to keep your decisions child-focused, keeping in mind that you and your co-parent may have different ideas about how to keep the decision-making focused on your children. Again, this doesn't mean one of you is wrong and the other is right; it simply means there are at least two ways to make the decision. For many co-parents, decision-making becomes a struggle for this reason. It's hard to see past what you believe is the right choice for your children.

If you're struggling to come up with ways to make decisions together for your children, here are a few ideas:

* Find common ground and build on that. Even the most contentious co-parents have common ground. It may take some work to find it, but do try.

- Think about how you would have made the decision if you were still married. Many times this removes any feelings of competition or disagreement and puts you in a collaborative mind-set.

- Take turns or split up making major decisions. You both have your children's best interests at heart, so if you cannot make decisions together, split them up, ensuring each parent has an opportunity to make decisions. One parent can handle medical while the other handles dental. One parent can sign the kids up for extracurricular activities while the other signs them up for school.

- Effectively communicate each of your goals within the decision. Many times conflict comes when each of the co-parents has a different primary goal. For example, you may want your children to participate in sports. Your co-parent may say they can only participate if they maintain good grades. If this leads to conflict, consider why each of you feel the way you do. Do you feel that sports are helpful to teach your children how to participate on a team? Does your co-parent feel that academic success weighs more than success within the team? Neither thought is wrong, but when you know what your goals are, you can more easily come to a compromise.

- Use a mediator or divorce coach who will guide you through the decision-making process. They'll look at both sets of opinions, work with you to brainstorm a variety of solutions, help you think through the outcomes of each solution, and guide you through to making a decision together.

One of the decisions that comes up for many parents is when children need braces. Generally speaking, a dentist is decided on, but it's only when the children are older that they need an orthodontist. If you can decide on an orthodontist early, this removes the decision later. If you want to wait to decide on an orthodontist later, come up with criteria to help you decide. What's important to you and your co-parent when it comes to health-care providers? Each of you should make a list of what's important to you so that when the time comes, it's easier for you to make a joint decision.

Besides decisions regarding health care, there are also everyday parental decisions. I discussed the importance of having similar rules and expectations in earlier chapters. This includes what consequences are rolled out. Parenting can be reactive instead of proactive, meaning you don't always know what behavior you'll have to correct until that behavior occurs. This is a good time to decide together how you'll manage behaviors across different houses. Even if it means "my house, my rules," make that decision together.

Think about how your life changed as you grew. Dating, jobs, and driving were all life experiences that came up later in the teen years. These are also experiences you'll want to think about with your co-parent. Do you have an age in mind when you and your co-parent will allow your children to date? How do you feel about part-time jobs in the teen years? Are you comfortable with your teenager learning to drive at age 16, or will you require certain grades before they're able to? Will they have to pay for driver's education or will you and your co-parent split the cost?

If your children are still young, these decisions may feel like they're a lifetime away, but they'll come up before you know it. If you and your co-parent have different ideas about how to handle these decisions, you will be conflicted later. Though you may not feel ready to make these decisions now, coming up with a way to make those decisions later will save you time and conflict and allow you to more quickly present a united front to your children.

Talk to friends or family members with older children. Ask them what came up as their children grew, and use this as a guideline to help you and your co-parent make decisions for later in your children's lives. If you don't already have a plan to communicate with your co-parent, make sure this is a part of it now. Communication is key to successful child-focused co-parenting. Without it, you and your co-parent are relying on guesswork and you'll have to reset every time your children are with you.

INCLUDING CHILDREN IN DECISIONS

One of the greatest tools parents have in their parenting arsenal is the ability to include their children in the decision-making process, where appropriate. This builds their self-esteem, makes them feel like a bigger part of your family, and teaches them problem-solving skills.

Sometimes children show that they're ready to be a part of decision-making by making their opinions on certain things clear. This can be anything from what to eat for dinner to whether or not they should have consequences for certain behavior. Use these clues to help you decide when and how to include them.

Give your children a voice in something small such as what the family will eat for dinner that evening. This shows them you're listening and puts their minds to work. Besides the fun decisions, many parents find that when they ask their children what their consequences should be for misbehavior, the children often give themselves a bigger consequence than what their parents had in mind! This shows the parents the lesson has been learned and gives them chance to be the "good guy" once in a while.

Ask yourself, "Is this a decision my child could make?" If the answer is yes, include them in the decision-making process.

Continue Building Your Relationship

The dust has settled on the divorce and on any new relationships that have formed. Your divorce is just a chapter in your children's lives. Just as you don't want your divorce to define you, you don't want it to define your children's adolescence either. Now is a great time to think about the bond you want to continue to build with your children and what steps you can take at each stage to do just that.

TODDLERS

Toddlers are such a fun group. They simply want someone on the floor playing with them. When you look at the world through the eyes of a toddler, you see it differently. Everything is new and exciting, and they want to share it with the people they're closest to. That's you!

Though playing on the floor doesn't always seem like the best use of time while laundry and dishes are piling up, your toddlers don't care about those things. They care about time with you. When they see you getting down on the floor and getting into their world, their confidence grows along with your relationship. The laundry will never go away, believe me, but your toddlers will grow out of this stage. Talk back to any voices in your head that make you feel guilty, and play!

You and your toddlers can also discover new things by going on a scavenger hunt in the park. Engage your senses together at a museum or petting zoo. Take the time to sit down and read together. Answer their many questions, and, if you don't know the answer, look it up together. Toddlers don't want to experience the things in life all alone; they want you along for the ride. You simply need to be present to experience it with them.

If there is one word preschoolers use more than any other, it's *why*. Why is the sky blue? Why do birds sing? Why do trains have whistles? Though it can be exhausting to have to answer so many "why" questions, your preschooler is trusting you for information, and it's a great start to strengthening your bond with them. Like toddlers, they want someone to play with and experience life with, but they also want to learn, and they're looking up to you for that.

If you're like many parents and are struggling with having to answer "why" one more time, think of it in a different way. What if you started a journal with as many of your preschooler's "why" questions and gave it to them as a keepsake when they graduated from high school? When you think of their questions as a memory builder, it makes it much easier to answer the next one. Their questions are a peek into who they're becoming. How much fun would it be to pull that journal out at graduation and remember some of the questions? You just may notice that those questions set your children on a path toward their career.

This is a perfect age to start game nights in your family. Your preschooler will learn taking turns, sharing, and how to lose, but most of all, they'll be having fun. Laughing with your children is one of the easiest ways to strengthen your bond, and game nights can be filled with laughter!

YOUNG CHILDREN

You can do so much with your school-aged children: game nights, movie nights, cook together, go for walks or ride bikes, play sports, or just about anything else you can think of. Your young children are capable and energetic and are waiting for you to take the lead. They want your attention. If they feel they don't have it, they may look for it in difficult ways. Many parents

I've worked with have mentioned to me that the behavior issues they'd been noticing in their children vanished as soon as they started paying a little extra attention to them.

Children at this age are much more independent and don't need quite as much as their younger counterparts. This frees you up to get more done, but it also separates you from your children. This is a great age to start scheduling regular time together. Whether it's simply family dinner a few times a month or a regular day of activity, the important part is making your children see that you have time for them and you want to enjoy that time. This sends an important message to your child that strengthens your bond.

One way you can spend time together is to include your children in your day-to-day activities. Cooking is one of the best ways to involve your children and get them to open up. The activity, which has to get done anyway, gives you a chance to build your bond. You can talk about your day, what's happening with their friends, and just generally catch up. This makes your children feel special and important, it's a chance to teach life skills, and you get one-on-one time with them.

PRETEENS

Preteens are all about showing their independence. It may not be "cool" to hang out with their parents anymore, but that doesn't mean they don't want to. Preteens still crave their parent's attention, but they don't want their parents to know it. Continue with your scheduled time together or start scheduling time together if you haven't already. Family time can grow as your children grow.

Get involved in their world a little by letting them choose the music for family game night. If they're watching YouTube nonstop, ask them to play some videos for you. If your preteen has found the latest fad, ask them about it. The last thing a pre-teen wants is to feel like their parents don't approve. If you get involved in their world and show interest in it, their self-esteem grows, as does your bond with them.

If you've already built some time together like cooking dinner, keep this going. If you haven't found that time, try watching a TV show with your children. TV time is something many families are doing anyway, but when you're doing it together, you are spending time together. Though it sounds counterintuitive, think about your favorite TV show. What happens when you learn that someone else watches it, too? Conversations usually come up immediately. The same can happen with your preteen. Building on your bond can be as simple as TV time together.

TEENAGERS

Your teenagers are planning for their life away from home, so this is the most important time to strengthen your bond. Find a show you can binge watch together, take them to sporting events, and build memories with your teenager that they'll take with them as they plan for and go off to college.

Teenagers are equal parts rewarding and difficult. Many parents tell me they're thrilled that they can finally have adult conversations with their teenagers but also say their teenagers aren't home to have those conversations! I've found that scheduling time with your teenagers is the easiest way to make sure you get to have those conversations. If you're having trouble finding time in your schedule, remember that teenagers love food. They may be much more motivated to schedule time if a meal is involved. You can build great memories with your teenager by trying various cuisines at different restaurants. Whatever you decide, know that even though your teenager doesn't always show it, they want you to spend time with them.

I asked my own teenagers about this section because building our bond is important to us. What they told me is that food is a major part of their lives, so even if we're getting a doughnut on a Saturday morning, they feel special. They also told me they want to be asked questions and to feel like they can talk about their lives. In fact, they said that some of their peers who don't have that type of relationship with their parents have expressed jealousy.

Teenagers don't always make it easy, but they definitely want to have a good relationship with you. Ask your teenager what they'd like to do and start there.

YOUNG ADULTS

Young adults are at a turning point in their lives. They're branching out on their own and learning what it's like to be out in the world. That's scary and exciting and strange. It's natural for them to turn to you more often than they did as teenagers and to lean on you a little more for your knowledge and life experience. You're their anchor! Many parents feel this is the stage in which their relationships with their children become more of a friendship and less of a parent-child relationship. You can share experiences and build on memories you've shared just as you would with a friend, but the bond is much stronger because you're family.

When it comes to strengthening your bond with your young adult, think about the things you would do with a friend and start to offer to do those things with your children. Would you spend a day antiquing? What about a day tailgating and watching a baseball game? Your children would probably love being part of these experiences and may not always have the funds to make it happen. You can make that possible for them. These are great memory-building, bond-strengthening experiences.

FIND TIME FOR FAMILY FUN

As your children grow and get involved in more things outside the home, it's hard to find the time to enjoy each other. That's why it's important to prioritize family time, too. How do you balance? Planning is your key to making time for activities that bring you together for several hours, but you don't need several hours to enjoy each other!

One family I worked with made a pact to laugh every day. They realized that there was so much pressure, especially during the busy sports seasons, that they would go days without laughing. It became a family "rule" to laugh before bed every day.

When the kids were young, they would simply play with each other, and before long they were laughing. A Nerf gun battle will bring out the smiles every time! When the kids grew, the parents used this opportunity to get into their children's love-of-all-things YouTube. The kids would find a different funny video to watch every night before bed. The kids loved feeling in charge of the funny video, and whenever the other members of their family laughed at the video *they* chose, they felt so proud of themselves! The parents loved the few minutes they spent watching these videos, and the entire family went to bed in a good mood, almost every night.

Of course, family dinners and vacations are important for bonding and enjoying each other, but if you get creative, you can find fun with just a few minutes of togetherness.

The hardest part of divorce is over! You've spent the time to transition and used the experiences learned during that time to revisit your parenting plan. Focusing on your bond with your children shows them how committed you are to family even after you've redefined it. You are showing your children that not all hard situations last; you're showing them how to manage and make the best of the situations and how to continue to build on the important relationships in life. Keep moving forward, knowing the work you do is strengthening your bond, as well.

Parenting Plan Checklist

Ideally, when you and your spouse decide to get divorced, you will begin working together to discuss and create your parenting plan. While this checklist is fairly comprehensive, every situation is different, so add important items to your parenting plan even if they are not mentioned here. Type up the plan, print it out, and allow room for both parents to sign it.

Depending on your situation and the status of your divorce, the parenting plan may be a document just for the two of you or it may be notarized and filed with the court. Perhaps a mediator witness will be present, or your lawyers will be involved. Whatever the case may be, the parenting plan is for the well-being of your children, so do your best to compromise with your co-partner and come to mutual agreements.

Scheduling

- School year parenting time
- Winter and spring break parenting time
- Holiday schedule
- Summer schedule
- Vacation time
- How will changes to the schedule be handled?

Communication

○ How will parents communicate (by phone, text, e-mail, co-parenting communication tool, or in person)?

○ What will be communicated?

○ Is there a time limit to respond?

○ Do children have access to their other parent by phone, video chat, or text? Should a time be set up to allow for this?

○ Will you set up a schedule for co-parent meetings through-out the year to discuss calendars, children's behaviors, and/or any other matters that can be addressed at that time?

Transportation

○ How will pickup and drop-off be handled?

○ What location?

○ Who will drive?

Health-Care Providers

Make sure each of the following are listed, as applicable:

○ Medical providers

○ Dental providers

○ Orthodontist

○ Specialists

○ Vision care

○ Psychologist/therapist/counselor

Financial

○ How will health-care bills (medical, dental, etc.) be split?

○ Will each parent be responsible for their own daycare for the children or will the cost be split?

○ How will school fees be split?

○ Will each parent be responsible for the children's clothing kept at their own home or will there be one budget for these items?

○ Who will pay for school supplies, hot lunches, and field trips?

Final Steps

○ Did both parents agree with or compromise to agree with the items listed?

○ Did both parents sign the agreement?

○ Does this agreement need to be notarized? Will a mediator witness this agreement? Will this agreement go through lawyers?

Going Forward

○ How will requests for changes to the parenting plan be handled?

○ What happens if a parent doesn't follow the parenting plan?

Resources

Divorce Help and Mediation

Karen Becker, MA: KarenBeckerLifeCoach.com

Divorce HQ/Collaborative Attorneys: DivorceHQ.com

Psychology Today/Divorce Therapists: PsychologyToday.com/us/therapists/divorce

Thumbtack/Mediators: Thumbtack.com/k/mediators

Co-Parenting Communication Tools

coparently: Coparently.com

Our Family Wizard: OurFamilyWizard.com

Parent Resources: Divorce and Separation. Mister Rogers Productions: FredRogers.org/parents/special-challenges/divorce.php

Talking Parents: TalkingParents.com

Parenting Professionals

Love and Logic: LoveAndLogic.com

Triple P Positive Parenting: TripleP.net/glo-en/home

Divorce-Related Videos for Children

Life's Little Lessons: A PBS Kids Learning Kit with Daniel Tiger—Separation: http://pbskids.org/learn/lifes-little-lessons/separation

Sesame Street Divorce Toolkit: SesameStreet.org/toolkits/divorce

Divorce-Related Books for Children

Brown, Marc, and Laurie Krasny Brown. *Dinosaurs Divorce: A Guide for Changing Families*. New York: Little, Brown and Company, 1986.

LeMaire, Colleen, and Marina Saumell. *I Have Two Homes*. North Charleston, SC: CreateSpace Independent Publishing Platform, 2014.

Masurel, Claire, and Kady McDonald Denton. *Two Homes*. Cambridge, MA: Candlewick Press, 2003.

Moore-Mallinos, Jennifer, and Marta Fàbrega. *When My Parents Forgot How to Be Friends*. Hauppauge, NY: Barron's Educational Series, 2012.

Winchester, Kent, and Roberta Beyer. *What in the World Do You Do When Your Parents Divorce? A Survival Guide for Kids*. Minneapolis, MN: Free Spirit Publishing, 2001.

References

American Psychological Association. "Marriage and Divorce." APA.org. Accessed July 16, 2018. www.apa.org/topics/divorce/.

Healy, Maureen. "Kids Feeling Blue? 5 Ways to Get Them Talking." Psychology Today. October 5, 2011. Accessed July 16, 2018. www.psychologytoday.com/us/blog/creative-development /201110/kids-feeling-blue-5-ways-get-them-talking.

KidsHealth from Neymours. "Talking About Your Feelings." KidsHealth.org. Accessed July 16, 2018. https://kidshealth.org /en/kids/talk-feelings.html.

Moyses, Kendra. "Help Young Children Identify and Express Emotions." Michigan State University Extension. July 15, 2013. Accessed July 16, 2018. msue.anr.msu.edu/news/help_young _children_identify_and_express_emotions.

Paris, Wendy. "Yes, You Can Raise Happy Children After Divorce: What Kids Really Need to Thrive." Psychology Today. March 17, 2015. Accessed July 16, 2018. www.psychologytoday .com/us/blog/splitopia/201503/yes-you-can-raise-happy -children-after-divorce.

Staley, Oliver. "Kids Need Structure More Than Warmth from Their Parents, According to a Top Child Psychologist." Quartz. Accessed July 16, 2018. https://qz.com/1039939/child-psychologist-lisa-damour-says-kids-need-rules-more-than-affection-from-their-parents/.

Tanner, Lindsey. "Self-Harm, Suicide Attempts Climb Among U.S. Girls, Study Says." Associated Press. STAT News. November 21, 2017. Accessed July 16, 2018. www.statnews.com/2017/11/21/self-harm-suicide-girls.

Vanderbilt University. "Teaching Your Child To: Identify and Express Emotions." The Center on the Social and Emotional Foundations for Early Learning. Accessed July 16, 2018. csefel.vanderbilt.edu/familytools/teaching_emotions.pdf.

Index

Acknowledgments

I am thankful to each of the families I have worked with in my practice. These families—and now you—are part of an important child-focused revolution. You're the example for positive co-parenting, even when it's hard.

Without my family, I would not be here. Jason, your support and patience made it possible for this book to happen. Tina, you are both an anchor and wind in my sails. Isabelle, Kacey, Jordan, and Kaylee—you are the reason I get up every morning and why I do what I do. You have all encouraged me and been patient with me throughout this process. I couldn't have done it without you.

To the team at Callisto Media, you are a force! You created this idea and stood beside me, providing me with professional support along the way to make it happen. You know the good you are putting into this world with this book. Thank you.

About the Author

KAREN BECKER is a family coach and divorced family coordinator. She has worked with hundreds of families one-on-one and in group settings as they've transitioned from parenting together to co-parenting in separate homes. Her own experiences as a co-parent as well as her education in counseling have helped her build curriculum, communicate techniques, and produce worksheets that help take the negative emotion out of the co-parents' relationship and put the focus on the children. From self-care techniques to communication tips and tricks to parenting issues, the families who have worked with Karen have all found better ways of handling life after divorce. Visit KarenBeckerLifeCoach.com.

CPSIA information can be obtained
at www.ICGtesting.com
Printed in the USA
LVHW020044181118
597498LV00025B/274/P